THE EASY
Italian Cookbook

THE EASY
Italian Cookbook

100 Quick and Authentic Recipes

PAULETTE LICITRA

Photography by Hélène Dujardin

ROCKRIDGE
PRESS

To my Mom,

*whose Italian cooking genius guides
me in the kitchen every day.*

Contents

Introduction

Italian cooking is one of the most loved cuisines in the world. And there are good reasons for that. The ingredients in Italian dishes are fresh, the recipes are uncomplicated, and the spirit behind Italian culture is warm and inviting. I'm second-generation Italian American. My grandparents came from Italy to New York City; my parents grew up in Brooklyn, and I was born in Brooklyn. My mother learned to cook from her mother, from her aunt, from her mother-in-law, and from our upstairs neighbor whom I called "Aunt Mary," a Sicilian friend who became my mom's mentor. Generations of recipes were passed from my mom's hands to mine. I've lived in Italy, where my Italian American heritage merged with Euro-Italian traditions and the everyday life of Italians. I've cooked alongside Italian home cooks in many regions of Italy. At home, I teach Italian cooking to my students, and also take them to Italy to experience the culture firsthand. The art of the Italian table has many layers. There is a spirit of giving, of cooking with tenderness and love, of sharing with family and friends, and of making an everyday meal a festive event. Dive into these recipes and become a member of the Italian table—because the soul of Italian culture is in its *food*.

Eat Like an Italian

The life of an Italian revolves around moments of eating. For breakfast, Italians keep it light: a quick espresso from their stovetop espresso pots and some crunchy bread or focaccia. But there's more happy munching before lunch. A mid-morning snack might be a fast piece of pizza from a take-out pizza stand, or maybe a *tramezzino*—a small sandwich-snack filled with mozzarella and tomato—from the corner "bar." By the time noon arrives, Italians are hungry again. Lunch, or *pranzo*, is the main meal of the day and often consists of two or more courses: *primo piatto* (first course)—pasta, soup, or risotto—and *secondo piatto* (second course)—meat, fish, or seafood. The meal is accompanied by *contorni*—vegetables like sautéed spinach or roasted potatoes. Lunch is typically capped with something sweet but simple, like fresh fruit. The irresistible pastries and cakes of Italy are usually reserved for special occasions or Sundays. Evening dinner is called *cena* and is not as big as lunch. A robust soup is a perfect *cena*. Italian home cooks buy food daily so that ingredients are always fresh. On Sunday afternoons, families gather at home or at special restaurants for long, luscious meals. Long conversations at the table are as much a part of the meal as the platters of sumptuous delights.

The Heart of Italian Cuisine

Italians have a reputation for being warm and welcoming, but they are also pragmatists, especially in the kitchen. This is what makes Italian cooking fully focused on seasonal ingredients. Why cook with an ingredient that isn't readily available? That wouldn't be very practical. So, when it's artichoke season, menus in restaurants and home kitchens are full of artichokes. When their season is over, artichokes disappear from the spotlight and the next seasonal star, like eggplant, takes the stage.

Using simple techniques, Italian home cooks create their recipes based on a few fresh ingredients and personal taste, and there's no shortage of variations. Ingredients are important, but the execution of recipes invites personalized input. Do you prefer more garlic? Would you like it to be spicier? Do you love lots of cheese? As you work your way through the dishes in this book, indulge in the cooking motto of Italian kitchens: *Quanto basta?* ("How much? Whatever *you* think is enough."). I developed these recipes with my own preferred balance of flavors in mind, based on my Italian American heritage and experiences cooking in Italy, but feel free to tweak them as you like. You'll find that each recipe in this book is easy to follow and fun to execute. I've identified those recipes that are dairy-free, gluten-free, vegetarian/vegan, one-pan, or quickly made in under 30 minutes, but check ingredient packaging to make sure the product you're buying doesn't contain any unexpected dairy, gluten, or meat.

As you master the straightforward methods of this style of cooking, you'll soon discover how easy it is to enjoy the enticing aromas and irresistible pleasures of Italian cuisine any night of the week.

Eggplant Parmigiana,
page 92

1

Italian Essentials

In this chapter, you'll learn about key staple ingredients that Italians incorporate into everyday dishes. Once you stock your kitchen with an assortment of these fresh vegetables, cheeses, cured meats, and pantry items, deliciously authentic home-cooked Italian meals are just minutes away. Since the recipes in this book create maximum flavor with minimal ingredients, it's worth it to buy high-quality products whenever possible. Trust me: You'll taste the difference.

Knowing Your Ingredients

Do not be overwhelmed by the length of this list; it is by no means a prompt to go out and buy all of these things at once. But it may be helpful to familiarize yourself with the principal ingredients of Italian cuisine before diving into the recipes.

Anchovies: You can find anchovies in small tins filled with oil or in jars imported from Italy. The fish are so small that processors don't even remove the bones before packing them into tins or jars, and their salty, assertive flavor makes a great base for sauces. Anchovy is also the distinctive ingredient in Caesar salad dressing (see page 37). In Italy, you will also find fresh anchovies that are bright white, filleted, marinated, and very mild in flavor.

Arugula: This salad green has a pleasing peppery taste. It's perfect in a salad all by itself, but wonderful, too, as part of a mixed salad with other lettuces. You'll often find baby arugula in stores (with leaves about 2 inches long), triple-washed and ready to go. Toss a few leaves on top of a cheesy crostini to add some green and crunch. In Europe, arugula is sometimes called "rocket," probably from the French *roquette*, also a type of arugula.

Basil: I think of basil as the national herb of Italy. Its deeply fragrant aroma and flowery, savory flavor seem to embody all of Italy. It originated in the Ligurian region, where it is called Genoese basil. Basil is one of the star ingredients in Neapolitan Pizza Margherita, along with buffalo mozzarella and San Marzano tomatoes, and this trio of ingredients represent the three colors of the Italian flag (green, white, and red). Basil is also the mainstay in traditional pesto. Note that this herb discolors when cut with a knife. When possible, tear the leaves with your fingers.

Bay leaves: I'll never forget the first time I met a fresh bay leaf. It came from a laurel tree in the backyard of a villa in the Italian Riviera. Bay leaves are laurel leaves. My hosts placed a two-foot laurel branch into their wood-burning, outdoor oven to flavor a beef roast. Bay leaves have a woodsy, old-world taste. You usually find them dried, but sometimes a specialty food market will carry fresh ones.

Beans: The two beans you often find in Italian dishes are cannellini beans and chickpeas (also known as garbanzo, or *ceci* in Italian). Cannellini are basically white kidney beans, but a little smaller and more delicate in flavor. They can be puréed as a spread for crostini, and they're a main ingredient in Pasta Fagioli with Cannellini Beans (page 28). Chickpeas shine in simple pasta dishes or on their own with onion and herbs.

Bread crumbs: This humble ingredient adds texture and flavor to countless Italian dishes, from hearty stuffing and meatballs to crunchy toppings. Buy unseasoned bread crumbs and add any flavoring you like. I love using panko bread crumbs for coating fish and meats before frying or baking, as panko's bigger crumbs create an especially satisfying crust.

Broth: The base of any risotto is a good broth. You can make your own broth by simmering chicken, meat, and/or vegetables in water, but if you don't have time, store-bought broth is a fine alternative. If you buy premade broth, make sure to choose a low-sodium brand so you can control the amount of salt in the finished dish.

Burrata: Though it looks like an unassuming ball of fresh mozzarella, when you cut into a ball of burrata, a creamy cascade of soft cheese spills forth. Burrata is perfect for spreading on a crusty slice of bread or serving with an antipasto platter. It also goes well with *salumi* and olives, and I love it as a topping for pizza. Burrata hails from the Puglia region of Italy, where it's made fresh daily.

Capers: Capers are flower buds that haven't yet opened. Their flavor is pungent and a bit sharp, like little pops of sunshine, and they are most famously grown in Pantelleria, an island off of Sicily. In the United States, capers are commonly sold brined in jars, but you can also find them packed with salt in cans at Italian specialty markets. I love them in tuna salad, mixed into mayonnaise, on roasted fish, and as the finishing touch for Chicken Piccata with Lemon and Capers (page 100).

Cornmeal: Centuries ago, when Italians first started growing corn, it was considered food for livestock. Corn is still used for livestock today, but along the way, Italians decided to mill the corn into a coarse or fine meal to cook like porridge. This cooked cornmeal is called polenta, and it is delicious paired with savory vegetables and meats. When you chill polenta, it thickens into a cake-like consistency. And in this thickened state, you can cut the polenta into slices and fry it in olive oil for another delicious variation. Though you can find products marketed as polenta at the grocery store, I get great results from simple (and much cheaper) cornmeal.

Escarole: In the spectrum of flavors, Italians have a particular affection for bitter. Escarole is one of those slightly bitter Italian greens, commonly used in Italian Wedding Soup with Mini Meatballs (page 29). I also love to use the pale-green inner leaves of raw escarole in salads. Escarole leaves have a denser crunch than lettuce, and they're buttery and slightly tangy in flavor.

Espresso coffee: Italian coffee is roasted until it is very dark—darker than a French roast. Every Italian family has a stovetop espresso pot for their morning coffee. These little metal pots last forever and are passed down through generations. Bialetti pots are the Italian favorite, and I love the Lavazza brand of coffee. Espresso is a key ingredient in Quick Tiramisu with Biscotti and Mascarpone (page 137).

Flour: Where would pasta and pizza be without flour? All-purpose flour is fine to use in the recipes in this book. But in Italy, the "all-purpose" flour you'll find in the markets, and on home-kitchen shelves, is labeled "00." *Doppio zero* (00) flour is more finely milled than American all-purpose flour, and it is made with a different type of wheat. If you find 00 flour, feel free to use it instead of all-purpose flour in equal proportions for the recipes in this book.

Garlic: In the south of Italy, garlic is used more often, and in more abundance, than in the north. Garlic has a great punch of flavor that's strongest when raw. Roasting and sautéing softens its strength and brings a more complex presence to a dish. I sauté whole cloves in the beginning of a tomato sauce, but then take the garlic out at the end. Contrary to popular belief, most Italians do not enjoy actual pieces of garlic in their food.

Grana Padano: The processing and drying process of Grana Padano cheese (as well as the flavor) is similar to that of its big brother Parmigiano-Reggiano, but Grana Padano is not aged as long, and regulations for its production are more relaxed. Cut it into chunks for snacking, or grate it finely to sprinkle over pasta or risotto.

Herbs: Fresh herbs are your best friend for almost any dish. Add them at the end as edible garnish, and you'll elevate your finished recipe without much fuss. Most herbs lose their essence when dried, winding up almost flavorless (like dried basil and parsley). But there are exceptions: both oregano and thyme become more intense in flavor when they are dried.

D.O.P.

You sometimes see this designation on Italian food product labels. It stands for *Denominazione di Origine Protetta*, which translates to "Protected Designation of Origin." Cheeses and cured meats such as Parmigiano-Reggiano and prosciutto di Parma, and even baked goods such as Altamura bread–can carry this classification. When you see "D.O.P." on a food label, you know that the product was produced in an official region of Italy and is not a copy manufactured in another country.

Lemons: Lemons grow to grapefruit size all over the region of Campania, Italy. So, of course, these citrus fruits have made their way into the recipes of that area, such as *limoncello*, a sweet, lemon-flavored after-dinner drink, and Amalfi Lemony Tuna Capellini (page 64). Lemons add a bright acidic element to many dishes, and lemon juice is the perfect Italian ingredient for salad dressings.

Mascarpone: I call mascarpone the cream cheese of Italy. It's not as tangy as American cream cheese, but it has a similar texture: dense and full-bodied. It's the rich ingredient in tiramisu and a fabulous addition to cheesecake. Mascarpone is originally from the Lombardia region in the north of Italy, where Milan is the capital. In general, cream and butter are more commonly used in northern Italy than in southern Italy.

Mozzarella: This mildly flavored white cheese comes in two different forms—fresh and low-moisture—and is typically made with cow's milk or the milk of water buffaloes raised in Italy (*mozzarella di bufala*). Fresh mozzarella is soft and wet, sold in balls either wrapped in plastic or floating in containers filled with water. Low-moisture mozzarella has a denser consistency and tangier, saltier flavor than fresh, and it is sold in blocks wrapped in plastic. I prefer the softer fresh mozzarella for snacking and baked pasta dishes. The harder low-moisture mozzarella is good for grating and sprinkling on pizza.

Nutmeg: Nutmeg is most often used in northern Italian cooking. The brightly pungent nut is lightly grated into cream sauces like béchamel, over risotto dishes, or into polenta. It's also used with butternut squash to flavor fillings for ravioli, and in very small doses in some desserts.

EXTRA-VIRGIN OLIVE OIL

EVOO: It's the foundation of almost all Italian cooking. Full of healthy antioxidants and high in monounsaturated fats, olive oil is the fundamental ingredient of a Mediterranean diet. Olive trees are abundant in Italy–especially in the region of Puglia. The flavor of olive oil is subtle, yet distinctive, and defines the character of Italian cooking. Extra-virgin olive oil is oil that is made from cold-pressed olives, extracted without heat or chemical processing. I cook with extra-virgin olive oil for everything (except for the occasional deep frying, when I use canola oil). Sometimes you'll see "boutique" extra-virgin olive oils in slim, pretty bottles. This oil tastes super-concentrated (and delicious). I wouldn't use it for everyday cooking, but more as a finishing oil, on salads, or as a dip for vegetables and bread. Everyday-use brands, like Colavita or California Olive Ranch, can be found in most supermarkets. But more often, I prefer the cost-value of some store brands, like Whole Foods 365, Traders Joe's President Reserve, and World Market Extra-Virgin Olive Oil. Sometimes, an extra-virgin olive oil that is packed in Italy can be a blend of oils from Spain, Greece, and Italy. The bottles are usually marked with this information.

Onions: These hearty alliums serve as flavor workhorses for many different dishes. Sautéed at the beginning of a tomato sauce, braise, or risotto, onions tend to melt from view but leave behind a perfect complexity and essence. In certain recipes, I like to swap out onions for one of their cousins, shallots or leeks. Both of these alternate alliums do the same job as onions, but they offer slightly different flavors.

Oregano: This is the first herb I ever learned to use in the first recipe I ever attempted on my own: dried oregano sprinkled on a tomato salad with olive oil and chopped onion. Most often used dried, oregano is a great pizza-flavor ingredient, and it is key to the taste of a tomato sauce meant to be served with seafood. Though it's more potent when dried, oregano is also excellent as a fresh herb.

Pancetta: I think of pancetta as the bacon of Italy. Pancetta is not smoked like bacon; it is simply cured pork belly seasoned with salt. You can sometimes get it sliced at deli counters, or sold already diced in packages. Just like bacon, it adds big flavor. Guanciale, which is closely related, is cured pig's cheek or jowl, and the featured ingredient in Spaghetti alla Carbonara on page 61. Guanciale and pancetta can be used interchangeably (as can bacon).

Parmigiano-Reggiano: It's right there in the name: true Parmigiano comes from Parma. The cheesemaking process for this classic Italian variety is generations-old and regulated by the government. Parmigiano is creamy, salty, a bit nutty, and can be eaten in chunks or grated over pasta. One important note: true Parmigiano-Reggiano is expensive, so I often opt for grated domestic Parmesan cheese instead. Certain American brands come close to the authentic taste (I recommend the Cello brand from Costco).

Parsley: Parsley is the herb "thread" that weaves through much of Italian cooking. It tastes *green*—you know it's in the dish, but it stands back and lets the other ingredients shine. Buy fresh Italian parsley, which is the flat-leaf variety. It has more flavor and is readily available in most supermarkets. Parsley makes appearances in meatballs and stuffing, and is sautéed in sauces and sprinkled on cooked meats, fish, and pastas. I also use it in pesto and salsa verde.

Pasta: Fresh pasta can be made with flour and eggs or just flour and water, depending on the region. In Sicily, they use semolina flour, which gives the pasta a slightly yellow tint. But most Italians use dry pasta—called *pastasciutta*—for their everyday meals. In the stores I like to buy pastas that are labeled "product of Italy." Italian producers use specific wheat varieties and mill their grains differently to create pastas that hold up well during cooking and don't become pasty.

Pecorino: Pecorino cheese is most often grated for pasta, in the same way as Parmigiano-Reggiano. But pecorino is sharper in flavor, a little saltier, and a favorite for many Roman pasta dishes like Spaghetti Cacio e Pepe (page 62). It's a sheep's milk cheese—*pecora* means sheep in Italian. Pecorino Romano is produced in the Lazio region, and Pecorinio Sardo is from the island of Sardinia. The longer they are aged, the sharper the flavor. Young pecorino is softer and creamier than longer-aged versions.

Peperoncino: This is the spicy pepper used to make the crushed red pepper flakes you find in shaker jars at most pizzerias. They're small red peppers, and, in home kitchens throughout Italy, you'll usually see a dozen or so strung together to hang and dry. Cooks can just break off a pod and crumble it into their dishes. The dried pepper and its seeds are fiery hot and the perfect ingredient to put a spicy edge on any dish.

Pine nuts: Pine nuts, or *pinoli*, grow in the center of pinecones from the *Pinus pinea* tree. When the pinecone drops and dries, and its scales open a bit, the tiny pine nuts fall out. At this stage they're coated in dark brown shells. It's not easy to get them out of these shells, and that's part of the reason why pine nuts are so expensive. Each little nut is an explosion of precious flavor. Use them in both savory and sweet dishes.

Prosciutto: This is a full hind leg of pork, salted, air-dried, and aged. The most traditional version is *Prosciutto di Parma* from the region of Emilia-Romagna. This Parma prosciutto has a D.O.P. designation, meaning that it is government checked to make sure the ham is from local pigs and is cured according to traditional standards. The cured version is called prosciutto *crudo* (meaning "raw"); the baked version, which is pink like boiled ham, is prosciutto *cotto*. Prosciutto is best when sliced paper thin. Its flavor is gentle, with both sweet and salty notes.

Rice: Italians have their own preferred rice varieties, some of which are grown right in Italy. The prized short-grain rice, arborio, is used in risotto and Italian rice dishes like Risi e Bisi (Venetian Rice and Peas) (page 45). Arborio has a dense starch center that is released during the constant stirring of the risotto process. This is what makes risotto so creamy. During cooking, arborio rice grains still maintain their structure; they don't become soft and mushy. Other Italian short-grain rice varieties are *carnaroli* and *vialone nano*.

Ricotta: This lush, creamy ingredient is a whey cheese, meaning that it's created using the leftover whey from the production of other cheeses. It's a favorite for ravioli fillings, lasagna, and other baked pastas. It's also the key element of the iconic Italian dessert cannoli. You can buy great-quality ricotta from any supermarket. My favorite brands are Polly-O and Galbani. Get the whole-milk variety, as it's richer and more authentic tasting.

Rosemary: The leaves of this herb look like pine needles; run your fingers over a sprig, and it will release a heady, evergreen aroma. Rosemary leaves are pretty hardy and don't break down during cooking. The best way to impart their earthy taste is to strip the leaves from the stem and mince them. Or you can add whole stems while cooking, then remove them just before serving so their beautiful rosemary essence will remain in the finished dish.

Saffron: This exotic spice is mostly used in Spanish cooking, but it's also the subtle ingredient in Milan's classic Risotto Milanese with Saffron (page 48). It gives the rice a pale-yellow color. Saffron ranges in color from deep red to dark orange. The thin, small threads are the stamens from a specific variety of crocus flower. That's why the spice is so costly; each tiny stamen has to be extracted by hand.

Sage: Pale, green-gray sage leaves feel a little fuzzy to the touch, and their gently aromatic flavor brings complexity and elegance to a variety of dishes. For Chicken Saltimbocca with Sage and Prosciutto (page 102), a whole leaf is attached to each meat medallion. Sage leaves are deep-fried for a crispy garnish, or added whole when roasting meats and vegetables. Sage and butter, heated together, makes a delicious quick sauce for pasta.

Salumi: Here is the catchall name for any Italian cured meat. A platter of *salumi* for, say, an antipasto, might have slices, rolls, or chunks of salami, cappocollo, prosciutto, mortadella, bresaola, speck, or soppressata. Every region has their own unique version of some or all of these types of cured meats.

Swiss chard: Known in Italy as *bietola*, Swiss chard is similar to spinach but with a slightly stronger and "greener" flavor. The large green leaves have white veins, but sometimes the veins are red or yellow. I usually cut out the tougher veins and stems and cook the torn leaves quickly in a little water and olive oil (see page 94).

Tomatoes: The most ubiquitous ingredients in the Italian pantry, aside from pasta, are tomatoes. Almost every recipe in this book that calls for tomatoes uses my favorite: crushed tomatoes from a can or jar. Crushed tomatoes have a pleasant thickness and are free of seeds and skins. You can also find canned San Marzano whole peeled tomatoes in major grocery stores. These much-lauded tomatoes are grown in the foothills of Mount Vesuvius near Naples.

Vinegar: The word for vinegar in Italian is *aceto*. A favorite way to preserve vegetables is *sotto'aceto*, which means "under vinegar," or pickled. Vinegar is also the partner of olive oil for a typical Italian salad dressing. The rule for basic vinaigrette is to use three parts olive oil to one part vinegar. Red wine and white wine are the most common types of vinegar, but balsamic vinegar holds a more revered place in Italian cuisine. Traditional balsamic vinegar (from the region of Emilia Romagna) is aged for at least 12 years, and is therefore very expensive. It's used sparingly, just in drops, to embellish risotto, creamy pasta dishes, or even gelato.

Negroni, page 14
The Antipasto Platter,
page 18

2

Aperitivi and Appetizers

When there's a chance to celebrate anything with food, Italians will gladly partake. Having a drink called an *aperitivo* before dinner is one of my favorite indulgences. It's the first stop on the way to supper—a means of readying your palate for the meal to come. It's usually lighter than hard liquor, and can include one or more of the signature, Italian-born vermouths and aperitifs. I love making these drinks at home, as their flavors have a way of transporting you right to Italy in your imagination (and it's much cheaper than buying a plane ticket).

The other before-dinner Italian tradition is antipasto, which means "before the meal." These are appetizers that open your palate and accompany your *aperitivo*. An antipasto can be as simple as a plate of sliced prosciutto or a few chunks of cheese. Or it can be a little more elaborate, like Clams Oreganata (page 20) or Stuffed Mushrooms with Shallots and Bread Crumbs (page 23). Altogether, this predinner tradition is not to be missed for the true Italian experience.

Campari and Soda

SERVES: 1 | **PREP TIME:** 5 minutes

The first time I saw someone drinking a Campari and Soda at a bar in Italy, my eyes popped. Campari is bright red in color. In a glass on the rocks, it looks like something from the moon. I had to try it. A word of warning: Campari has a distinctly bitter taste and is therefore not for everyone. However, I took to it pretty fast.

½ cup ice cubes

2 ounces Campari

5 ounces club soda

Thin half slice of lemon

Place the ice cubes in a rocks glass or highball glass. Add the Campari, then the club soda; stir once to combine. Gently rub the lemon slice along rim of glass, then drop it into the drink.

INGREDIENT TIP: Campari was invented in 1860 by Gasparo Campari and was originally meant to be an after-dinner *amaro*. *Amaro* means "bitter" in Italian, and after-dinner drinks, called *digestivi*, are meant to aid in digestion (bitter flavors are thought to help with this process). So, try Campari after dinner, too. And as an *aperitivo*, switch out the club soda for tonic water—new great taste, new great drink.

PAIR WITH: Crispy Artichoke Hearts with Aioli Dip (page 19)

Aperol Spritz

SERVES: 1 | **PREP TIME:** 5 minutes

Aperol is a bright orange, lightly alcoholic beverage. The Aperol Spritz is an *aperitivo* of choice in the Italian city of Venice. And although it has a bright, summery personality, it's served all year round. The drink was created in the early twentieth century by the Barbieri brothers from the nearby town of Padua, and the recipe has remained the same ever since.

½ cup ice cubes

1 ounce Aperol

3 ounces Prosecco

½ ounce club soda

1 orange slice

Fill a stemmed wineglass halfway with ice. Pour in the Aperol, Prosecco, and club soda. Stir gently to combine. Cut a slit in the orange slice and wedge it onto the rim of the glass. Serve.

VARIATION TIP: Prosecco is like a light, not-so-dry champagne. You can switch out Prosecco in this drink for another sparkling wine if you like.

PAIR WITH: White Bean and Sage Crostini (page 21)

Negroni

SERVES: 1 | **PREP TIME:** 5 minutes

The Negroni is a drink named after an Italian count, Camillo Negroni. It's a genius combination blending the punch of gin, the softness of sweet vermouth, and a shot of bitter and bright Campari. Vermouth is a fortified wine with herbal and even floral hints. Sweet vermouth is red and is also a fine drink on its own, chilled, or on ice.

½ cup ice cubes

1 ounce gin

1 ounce sweet vermouth

1 ounce Campari

Thin sliver of orange peel

Fill a rocks glass with ice. Add the gin, sweet vermouth and Campari. Stir to combine. Lightly rub the orange peel around the rim of the glass, then drop it into drink.

VARIATION TIP: For a lighter version of this drink, try a Negroni *Sbagliato. Sbagliato* means mistake—as if you'd made the drink incorrectly. For Negroni *Sbagliato*, switch out the same amount of gin with bubbling prosecco instead.

PAIR WITH: The Antipasto Platter (page 18)

Peach Bellini

SERVES: 1 | **PREP TIME:** 5 minutes

The traditional Peach Bellini is made with puréed fresh white peaches. However, since it's not that easy to find fresh white peaches, in this recipe I've opted for peach nectar that you can buy in a jar or canned. The Bellini was invented at Harry's Bar in Venice. Every time I'm in Venice, I make sure to go to Harry's on the Grand Canal, sit at their bar in the beautiful, wood-paneled room, and sip a Bellini. It's the quintessential Venetian experience.

1 ounce peach nectar

2 ounces cold Prosecco

1 maraschino cherry

Pour the peach nectar into a champagne flute. Add the cold Prosecco, drop in the maraschino cherry, and serve.

VARIATION TIP: If you have a food processor, you can make a raspberry variation of the Bellini. Pulse ½ cup fresh raspberries with 2 teaspoons sugar and 2 teaspoons water until smooth. Then, stir in 2 cups cold prosecco. This amount serves 4.

PAIR WITH: Bruschetta with Honey Ricotta and Prosciutto (page 22)

Americano

SERVES: 1 | **PREP TIME:** 5 minutes

Despite its name, this *aperitivo* is decidedly Italian. Some people think it's called an Americano because the strength of the ingredients is diluted with club soda—making it more palatable for out-of-towners. Sweet vermouth also tempers the bitterness of Campari. Whatever the history behind this recipe, it's a wonderfully refreshing predinner drink.

½ cup ice

1 ounce Campari

1 ounce sweet vermouth

2 ounces club soda

1 thin slice lemon peel

Fill a highball glass with ice. Add the Campari, sweet vermouth, and club soda. Gently rub the lemon peel along the rim of the glass, then drop it into the drink.

PAIR WITH: Stuffed Mushrooms with Shallots and Bread Crumbs (page 23)

||||||||||||||||||||||||||||||||||||||||||||||||||||||||||||||||||||||||||||||||||||||||||

THE ART OF THE *APERITIVO*

There are "bars" all over Italy, but they may not resemble the bars that you are familiar with. The main beverage at these establishments is coffee—in all its forms—with a full complement of alcohol also on hand. Before dinner, Italians congregate at bars around 7 p.m. or so to relax with friends and an *aperitivo*—a light drink with some nibbles or snacks. Italy produces many types of liquor distinctly for *aperitivi*: Aperol, Campari, Punte e Mes, sweet and dry vermouth, and Carpano Bianco are just a few. Prosecco, a light bubbling wine, is also a favorite *aperitivo*. Sitting at a café table with your *aperitivo* and complimentary dish of olives or chips, you can watch the Italian world go by as you savor each individual taste. Then, after maybe an hour or so, it's time to go to dinner, which Italians enjoy late, around 9 p.m. Once, when I was in the region of Lombardia, we visited with friends at a bar before dinner. It took more than two hours for everyone to gather, and then we traveled another half hour to a special restaurant on top of a hill where we had dinner around 10:30 p.m. A normal evening in Italy.

||||||||||||||||||||||||||||||||||||||||||||||||||||||||||||||||||||||||||||||||||||||||||

Venetian Scroppino

SERVES: 4 | **PREP TIME:** 10 minutes

The small group I brought to Venice a few years ago took a cooking class with Chef Marika on the beautiful island of Lido. While we prepared a full Venetian feast, she prepared the Venetian Scroppino for us. It's a little like a frosty milkshake, but lemony and spiked with Prosecco. The drink is not well known outside of Venice, but it works well as an *aperitivo* or an after-dinner dessert drink no matter where you are.

2 cups vanilla ice cream, slightly softened

2 cups lemon sorbet

½ cup lemon-flavored soda (preferably Italian limonata)

½ cup chilled Prosecco

1. Combine the ice cream and sorbet in a large mixing bowl. Whisk vigorously until the mixture is smooth and creamy.

2. Gently whisk in the lemon soda and Prosecco until well combined.

3. Ladle the drink into 4 stemmed wineglasses. Serve immediately with straws.

TIME-SAVING TIP: If you have an immersion blender, you can make short work of blending all the ingredients at once. For the lemon soda, feel free to use Sprite or Fresca.

PAIR WITH: Parmigiano Crackers (page 81)

The Antipasto Platter

SERVES: 4 to 6 | **PREP TIME:** 20 minutes

This is probably the most common appetizer in Italy. The parts and pieces can change from day to day, but cured meats, some cheese, and some vegetables are always the main players. It's meant to be assembled on a large platter for eaters to pick on while sipping some wine or *aperitivi*. You can get as creative as you'd like, but this recipe results in a tried-and-true arrangement. For consistent slices, have your local deli counter prepare the meats for you.

¼ pound salami, thinly sliced

¼ pound prosciutto, thinly sliced

¼ pound capocollo or mortadella, thinly sliced

¼ pound provolone or Asiago cheese, cut into bite-size cubes

½ cup black or green olives

1 cup marinated artichoke hearts (from a jar)

½ cup grape tomatoes

4 to 5 basil leaves, torn

1 small loaf Italian bread, sliced

1. Use a large platter for the antipasto. Roll the salami, prosciutto, and capocollo (or mortadella) into tight rolls. Lay them out in one layer on one end of the platter.

2. Next to the meat, pile up the cheese cubes.

3. Arrange the olives next to the cheese, then add the artichokes and grape tomatoes.

4. Sprinkle the basil leaves on top, and serve the platter with the sliced bread alongside.

INGREDIENT TIP: The array of Italian cured meats available at most deli counters can be a bit daunting, but the best way to learn about them is to try them. Prosciutto has a buttery texture; capocollo is a bit like a denser ham, but with more fat in the slice (and more flavor). Mortadella has a bologna-like consistency.

PAIR WITH: Quick Bread Loaf with Ricotta and Ham (page 85)

Crispy Artichoke Hearts with Aioli Dip

SERVES: 4 to 6 | **PREP TIME:** 15 minutes | **COOK TIME:** 10 minutes

When these fried artichoke hearts appear on my mom's table, they are gone in a flash. I quickly adopted her recipe and made it my own. Artichokes have a strong umami content. Umami is the fifth flavor—sweet, sour, salty, and bitter are the other four. Umami means the food has an inherently tasty, super-savory quality. Use frozen artichoke hearts for this recipe, rather than canned or from a jar (I like Trader Joe's brand).

½ cup flour

Salt

Freshly ground
black pepper

2 eggs

12 ounces frozen
artichoke hearts, thawed
and patted dry

3 or 4 tablespoons
extra-virgin olive oil

½ cup mayonnaise

2 or 3 tablespoons freshly
squeezed lemon juice

1 small garlic clove, minced

1. Place the flour in a medium bowl and season to taste with salt and pepper. In a separate bowl, lightly beat the eggs.

2. Toss artichoke hearts in the seasoned flour. Working one at a time, remove the artichokes from the flour, shake off any excess flour, and dip them in the egg. Place the coated artichokes on a plate near the stove.

3. Heat the oil in a medium skillet over medium-high heat. When hot, add the coated artichokes, working in batches, and cook until they are golden, 2 to 3 minutes per side. Drain the artichokes on a paper-towel-lined plate. Season lightly with salt.

4. Combine the mayonnaise, lemon juice, and garlic in a small mixing bowl. Serve this sauce with the artichokes for dipping.

VARIATION TIP: My mother uses self-rising flour for this recipe. If you have some in the house, try it. It changes the outcome slightly. The finished artichoke hearts seem to be more neatly enclosed in the coating. Either way is great. These fried hearts are also fine on their own without the aioli.

PAIR WITH: Puff Pastry Pizza (page 80)

Clams Oreganata

SERVES: 4 to 6 | **PREP TIME:** 20 minutes | **COOK TIME:** 5 minutes

I grew up on the south shore of Long Island, New York. We used to go clamming at the beaches and bring the bivalves home super-fresh. My family loved experimenting with different ways of preparing clams; we would sometimes even eat them raw, right from the shell. This recipe has a few more steps than usual, but it's so worth it. Clams Oreganata is a classic Italian American appetizer. They're simpler than baked clams, and it's the easiest way to cook and flavor clams on the half-shell.

2 cloves garlic, peeled and minced

5 or 6 fresh Italian parsley sprigs, leaves minced

1¼ cup plain bread crumbs

¼ cup extra-virgin olive oil, plus more for drizzling

Salt

Freshly ground black pepper

2 dozen littleneck clams

3 tablespoons unsalted butter

1. Preheat the broiler.

2. In a medium mixing bowl, combine garlic, parsley, bread crumbs, and olive oil. Season with about ½ teaspoon salt and some black pepper to taste. Mix to combine well. Reserve.

3. Rinse the clams under cold water to get rid of any sand or grit. Add a little water to a large frying pan. Place clams in one layer. Cover and heat on medium for about 2 minutes, until the shells pop open. The aim is not to cook the clams completely, just to get the shells to open.

4. Remove clams from the pan; let cool until you can handle them. Open shell all the way, scrape clam into bottom half of the shell, and twist off the top shell (discard top shells). Slip a paring knife under each clam in the shell to loosen from shell, but leave clam in shell.

5. Line up clams on a sheet pan in one layer. Pat a spoonful of bread crumb mixture on top of each clam and tamp down. Cut small pieces of butter to top each clam. Broil clams (with pan 3 to 5 inches from broiler) about 5 minutes, until the bread crumbs are browned and crispy. Serve hot.

INGREDIENT TIP: When buying clams, look for the littleneck clams, which are smaller clams. When steaming them, you may find some that don't open. Steam these clams a little longer on their own, and if they still don't open, discard them.

PAIR WITH: Aperol Spritz (page 13)

White Bean and Sage Crostini

SERVES: 4 to 6 | **PREP TIME:** 15 minutes | **COOK TIME:** 5 minutes

This cannellini bean crostini is a classic Tuscan recipe. Crostini are typically small rounds of lightly toasted baguette bread—perfect mini-platforms for flavorful toppings. Consider having a crostini party with a variety of toppings: white bean and sage, chopped tomatoes, sautéed mushrooms, roasted peppers . . . the possibilities are endless.

1 small baguette

4 or 5 tablespoons extra-virgin olive oil, divided

1 (15-ounce) can cannellini beans

1 garlic clove, minced

Leaves from 3 to 4 sprigs fresh sage, minced

Salt

Freshly ground black pepper

1 tablespoon minced fresh Italian parsley

1. Preheat the oven to 375°F.

2. Slice the baguette into thin (¼-inch) slices. Place in one layer on a sheet pan. Brush lightly with a couple of tablespoons olive oil. Toast in oven until very lightly colored, about 5 minutes.

3. Empty the can of beans into a colander and rinse. Shake off excess water and pour beans into a medium mixing bowl. Using a potato masher, mash beans until well broken up, but still a little chunky. Add the remaining olive oil, garlic, and sage. Season with salt and pepper. Stir vigorously to combine. Add a bit of oil or water if mixture is too thick.

4. Spread a tablespoon or so on each crostini. Sprinkle with minced parsley. Serve.

TIME-SAVING TIP: If you have a food processor, you can make this recipe in less time and with a smoother texture. Simply pulse the beans, garlic, sage, olive oil, salt, and pepper in the food processor until smooth.

PAIR WITH: Negroni (page 14)

Bruschetta with Honey Ricotta and Prosciutto

SERVES: 4 to 6 | **PREP TIME:** 15 minutes | **COOK TIME:** 7 minutes

Sometimes people think "bruschetta" only refers to the typical bruschetta topping of chopped fresh tomatoes. However, *bruscare* means "to toast" in Italian, and so bruschetta (pronounced brew-sketta), refers to the toasted bread—no matter what topping is on it. Different from the small rounds of crostini, here we have a more generous slice of crunchy Italian bread. Bruschetta is typically grilled, but it is just as wonderful toasted.

FOR THE BRUSCHETTA

1 loaf of Italian bread, cut into ½-inch slices

3 or 4 tablespoons extra-virgin olive oil

2 garlic cloves, peeled and halved

Salt and freshly ground black pepper

FOR THE TOPPING

1 15-ounce container of ricotta

2 tablespoons honey

1 teaspoon salt

¼ pound prosciutto, thinly sliced

TO MAKE THE BRUSCHETTA

1. Preheat the oven to 375°F.
2. Lay bread slices in one layer on a sheet pan. Brush lightly with olive oil. Rub cut sides of garlic onto top side of each slice. Season lightly with salt and pepper. Toast in oven until golden, about 5 minutes.

TO MAKE THE TOPPING

In a medium mixing bowl, combine ricotta, honey, and salt. Mix well to combine.

TO FINISH DISH

Spread a layer of ricotta on each slice of toasted bread. Rip the slices of prosciutto into smaller pieces, and add a few strips on top of each ricotta-topped bruschetta. Serve.

INGREDIENT TIP: In Italy you often see bruschetta toasted to the point of being charred. Feel free to get some char when baking, or if you have a grill, grilled bruschetta is rustic goodness.

PAIR WITH: Campari and Soda (page 12)

Stuffed Mushrooms with Shallots and Bread Crumbs

SERVES: 4 to 6 | **PREP TIME:** 10 minutes | **COOK TIME:** 25 minutes

When you serve these stuffed mushrooms, everyone will be impressed with how sophisticated they look, but the truth is they couldn't be simpler to cook. The recipe calls for large white mushrooms, but you can use cremini (baby portobello), and also mix the sizes (like the various sizes you get in an 8-ounce package). That way some mushrooms will be a mouthful, and others will be cute little pops of flavor.

12 large white mushrooms

2 tablespoons extra-virgin olive oil, plus more for drizzling

1 shallot, peeled and minced

2 or 3 sprigs fresh Italian parsley, minced

¾ cup bread crumbs, preferably panko

Salt

Freshly ground black pepper

1. Preheat the oven to 400°F.

2. Rinse the mushrooms briefly in cool water to clean off any loose dirt. Pat dry. Remove and mince the stems.

3. Heat 2 tablespoons olive oil in a medium sauté pan. When hot, add the minced mushroom stems and minced shallot. Cook for 2 to 3 minutes, until the shallot softens. Add the parsley and bread crumbs. Stir until the bread crumbs absorb some olive oil, about 1 minute. Season lightly with salt and pepper.

4. Line a baking pan with foil. Drizzle it with a thin layer of olive oil. Place the mushroom caps upright on pan and season lightly with salt. Drizzle lightly with olive oil. Using a small spoon, fill each cap with filling.

5. Roast for 15 to 20 minutes until mushrooms have cooked through and topping is golden. Serve warm.

TIME-SAVING TIP: If you're having company, you can cook these stuffed mushrooms earlier in the day and reheat them right before serving. Or you can get them to the just-filled stage, refrigerate them, and then bake them in the oven for 20 minutes before company arrives.

PAIR WITH: Red and Green Pepper Frittata (page 42)

Sicilian Orange and Fennel Salad, page 33

3

Soups and Salads

Almost all of the Italian soups in this chapter are considered *di magro*, which means lean, or without meat, magically transforming pantry items into delicious, warming meals (as in Stracciatella (Italian Egg Drop Soup) on page 31, which calls for just eggs, grated Parmesan, and broth). Pair a soup with a great salad, and you have an entire meal. And take note: When it comes to salad, there are no bottled dressings in Italy. Olive oil with vinegar or lemon juice is the mainstay salad seasoning. There are exceptions, though, such as Caesar Salad (see page 37). This Italian American creation adds anchovy and grated Parmesan to the usual oil and vinegar dressing. Salads are often served at the end of the meal in Italy, as they are considered helpful for digestion.

Tuscan Ribollita (Hearty Vegetable and Bread Soup)

SERVES: 4 to 6 | **PREP TIME:** 20 minutes | **COOK TIME:** 45 minutes

Ribollita is a Tuscan classic that seems more like vegetable stew than a soup. Its high nutritious value is embedded in satisfying flavor. I first tasted this comforting soup at a small, tucked-away trattoria in Florence. It makes you instantly feel like a Florentine citizen. Don't let the ingredient list daunt you—half of the ingredients are staples that may already be in your kitchen.

2 or 3 tablespoons
extra-virgin olive oil,
plus extra for brushing

1 medium onion, diced

2 carrots, peeled and diced

2 celery stalks,
trimmed and diced

1 or 2 garlic cloves,
peeled and smashed

1 or 2 sprigs fresh rosemary,
leaves removed and minced

1 15-oz can plum tomatoes,
roughly cut up

1 15-oz can cannellini
beans, drained and rinsed

3 or 4 cups low-sodium
vegetable or chicken broth

4 or 5 cups green kale or
Tuscan (lacinato) kale,
torn into bite-size pieces

Salt

Freshly ground
black pepper

8 to 12 slices Italian
bread or baguette

½ cup grated Parmesan

1. Preheat the oven to 375°F.

2. Heat the olive oil in a large saucepan. When hot, add the onion, carrots, and celery. Cook until softened, but not browned, about 3 to 4 minutes. Add garlic and rosemary, and cook a minute or two more.

3. Add the tomatoes and beans; sauté for a couple of minutes. Add the broth. Season with salt and pepper. Bring to a simmer, then add the kale. Simmer for about 30 minutes until all the flavors combine.

4. Meanwhile, lay bread slices on a baking sheet in one layer. Brush or drizzle with a little olive oil; season with salt and pepper. Dust with 2 or 3 tablespoons grated Parmesan. Toast bread in oven until golden, 5 to 7 minutes.

5. To serve: Place a slice of bread in an individual soup bowl. Ladle soup on top. Top with another toast. Drizzle a little olive oil and dust with grated cheese. Serve hot.

INGREDIENT TIP: Regular green kale is fine in this recipe, but if you can find Tuscan (i.e., lacinato) kale, it makes the soup that much more authentic.

PAIR WITH: Cast Iron Pan Pizza Margherita (page 78)

Tortellini in Brodo with Spinach

SERVES: 4 to 6 | **COOK TIME:** 15 minutes

Brodo is Italian for broth, and as the recipe title suggests, this dish, hailing from the Emilia-Romagna region of Italy, couldn't be easier. It's perfect comfort food. You can buy fresh tortellini—usually filled with cheese—in the refrigerator section of your supermarket.

1 quart low-sodium vegetable or chicken broth

½ pound fresh tortellini

5 or 6 ounces baby spinach, rinsed

Salt

Freshly ground black pepper

⅓ cup grated Parmesan cheese

1. Heat broth in a large saucepan until simmering. Add tortellini and simmer 2 to 3 minutes.

2. Add spinach, simmer 1 minute, or until the spinach has wilted, and then season with salt and pepper to taste.

3. Serve hot, sprinkling some grated Parmesan over each bowl.

VARIATION TIP: You don't need to wait until you have tortellini on hand to make this. Any small pasta—like pastina or orzo—can be used instead; just simmer the pasta in the broth until it's al dente.

PAIR WITH: Parmigiano Popovers (page 82)

BASIC BROTH

In many restaurant kitchens, you'll find a tall, deep pot of water and vegetable scraps (onion skins, carrot shavings, leek tops, and celery leaves) constantly simmering on the back burner of the stove to make flavorful homemade vegetable broth. This method can also be used to make chicken broth with either chicken pieces or the carcass of a chicken with just its bones and any leftover meat. Broth brings a deeper flavor to a dish than water alone, and it adds extra nutrients, too. All broths should be simmered for as long as possible–ideally no less than 2 hours. In Italian cooking, broth is vital for soups and risotto.

I'm often asked, "What is the difference between broth and stock?" Typically, broth is seasoned with salt, uses meat rather than bones, and simmers for less time than stock. Either way, you end up with a very tasty liquid. Often, no one has time to make broth or stock, so there are lots of packaged broths at the supermarket. I rely on these to save time in the kitchen. If you are buying premade broth, choose low-sodium versions whenever possible, and adjust your seasonings accordingly, as even low-sodium broth can be a little salty.

Pasta Fagioli with Cannellini Beans

SERVES: 4 to 6 | **PREP TIME:** 10 minutes | **COOK TIME:** 20 minutes

Growing up in my Italian American household, we always called this dish "beans and macaroni." It's a comfort classic from the catalog of *cucina povera*, recipes that need just a few staples to make. This recipe contains no meat, but the beans fill the protein role, making this dish tasty, filling, and nutritious.

Salt

½ pound small-cut macaroni, i.e., elbow or ditalini

1 (15-ounce) can cannellini beans

Freshly ground black pepper

¼ cup extra-virgin olive oil

3 garlic cloves, peeled and cut in half

Leaves from 3 or 4 sprigs Italian parsley, minced

½ cup grated Parmesan cheese, for serving

1. Fill a large saucepan with 2 quarts water and bring to a boil. Season water with ½ tablespoon salt and pour in pasta. Cook until al dente (done but not mushy).

2. Meanwhile, drain and rinse the beans. Place the beans in a small saucepan, add 1½ cups of water, and season with salt and pepper. Bring to a simmer and cook for 2 to 3 minutes. Then shut off, and, using a potato masher, mash down the beans until some are smashed, but there are still some intact.

3. In another small saucepan, add the olive oil and garlic. Heat gently until the garlic gets just a little golden, then shut off.

4. Drain the pasta. Add pasta to a medium serving bowl. Add the beans and water. Add the olive oil and garlic. Sprinkle with parsley; toss to combine. Serve in bowls. Pass grated Parmesan for individual servings.

VARIATION TIP: For even more flavor, you can use broth instead of water in this recipe, although water is the typical ingredient.

PAIR WITH: Riviera Focaccia with Rosemary and Olives (page 83)

Italian Wedding Soup with Mini Meatballs

SERVES: 4 to 6 | **PREP TIME:** 30 minutes | **COOK TIME:** 40 minutes

Turns out, Italian wedding soup has nothing to do with weddings. It's all about "wedding" the flavors of meat, vegetables, and pasta. And that marriage gets even better the next day, so save some for leftovers. Since no Italian cookbook would be complete without this classic (but time-consuming) soup, I've pared down the process to make it more manageable.

FOR THE MEATBALLS

2 slices white bread

⅓ cup milk

1 pound ground beef

1 egg

⅓ cup grated Parmesan cheese

Handful fresh Italian parsley leaves, chopped

FOR THE SOUP

2 tablespoons extra-virgin olive oil

1 small onion, diced

2 carrots, diced

2 celery stalks, diced

2 garlic cloves, minced

6 cups low-sodium chicken or vegetable broth

Salt

Freshly ground black pepper

1 cup ditalini or other small pasta

12 to 16 ounces escarole leaves, cut into bite-size pieces

½ cup grated Parmesan cheese, for serving

TO MAKE THE MEATBALLS

1. Preheat the oven to 375°F. Line a rimmed baking sheet with foil or parchment paper.

2. Gently tear the crusts off the bread slices and discard crusts. Break up the white middles into small pieces, place them in a small bowl, and cover with the milk. Let sit for a couple of minutes, then pull up the soaked bread from the milk and transfer it to a large mixing bowl, along with the beef, egg, cheese, and parsley. Mix with your hands or a spoon until well combined.

3. Using your hands, roll the meat mixture into 1-inch balls and line them up on the prepared baking sheet. Bake until the meatballs are cooked through and golden, about 30 minutes.

TO MAKE THE SOUP

1. Heat the oil in a large saucepan and sauté the onion, carrots, and celery until softened. Add the garlic and cook for 1 minute more, until fragrant. Pour in the broth and season with salt and pepper to taste.

2. Simmer the soup for about 10 minutes, then add the pasta and cook until the pasta is al dente. Add the escarole and meatballs. Cook until the escarole is wilted, about 5 minutes more. Serve in individual bowls sprinkled with the grated cheese.

INGREDIENT TIP: Most supermarkets carry escarole year-round. It looks like a head of romaine lettuce, but the leaves are thicker and only curly on the ends, and it has a slightly bitter taste. If you can't find escarole, spinach is also very good in this soup.

PAIR WITH: Caesar Salad with Garlic-Anchovy Dressing (page 37)

Pappa al Pomodoro (Tomato and Bread Soup)

SERVES: 4 to 6 | **PREP TIME:** 20 minutes | **COOK TIME:** 35 minutes

Leave it to the Italians to make a spectacular soup out of bread. I wish I had been in that kitchen when Pappa al Pomodoro was invented. Stale bread was at hand, and so were tomatoes. With the added flavor of garlic and root vegetables, its authentic flavor will transport you to the Tuscan countryside.

3 tablespoons olive oil, plus more for drizzling

3 carrots, peeled and finely diced

2 celery stalks, finely diced

1 medium onion, finely diced

2 garlic cloves, minced

1 medium loaf peasant bread or ciabatta

1 (28-ounce) can peeled Italian tomatoes

3 cups low-sodium vegetable or chicken broth

½ cup red wine

Salt

Freshly ground black pepper

Handful fresh Italian parsley and/or basil leaves

½ cup grated Parmesan or Parmigiano-Reggiano cheese

1. Heat 3 tablespoons olive oil in a large saucepan. Sauté the carrot, celery, onion, and garlic until softened, 3 to 4 minutes.

2. Break open the loaf of bread and tear out the white inside of the bread (reserve crusts). Pull apart white part of bread into small pieces. Add to the sautéing vegetables. Stir until bread has absorbed some of the oil.

3. Open the can of tomatoes, and, using a pair of kitchen scissors, roughly cut the tomatoes. Add tomatoes to the pot with the vegetables and bread.

4. Add the broth and red wine. Season with salt and pepper. Bring to a simmer, and simmer uncovered, stirring often, pressing bread to break it up, for about 30 minutes until bread breaks down and flavors combine.

5. Meanwhile, preheat the oven to 375°F. Tear apart the reserved crusts of the bread into bite-size pieces. Lay them out on a sheet pan. Season with salt and pepper, drizzle a little olive oil over bread, and scatter the parsley or basil. Toast in oven for about 5 minutes. Remove from oven.

6. Ladle soup into serving bowls. Add some toasted pieces of bread, a drizzle of olive oil, and some grated Parmesan to each bowl.

TIME-SAVING TIP: You can leave out the crispy bread topping at the end if you don't have time. I love to add this crusty garnish, but the soup's not traditionally served that way.

PAIR WITH: Spice-Rubbed Pork Tenderloin (page 106)

Stracciatella (Italian Egg Drop Soup)

SERVES: 4 to 6 | **PREP TIME:** 10 minutes | **COOK TIME:** 5 minutes

When you need something hot, delicious, and nutritious—and you need it quickly—here's your dish. *Stracciatella* means "torn pieces," which is what the egg mixture looks like when it is cooked in the broth.

4 large eggs

½ cup grated Parmesan cheese, plus more for serving

½ teaspoon salt

¼ teaspoon freshly ground black pepper

Leaves from 3 or 4 sprigs fresh Italian parsley, minced

Pinch grated nutmeg (optional)

4 cups low-sodium vegetable or chicken broth

1. In a medium mixing bowl, beat the eggs together with grated Parmesan, salt, pepper, parsley, and nutmeg, if using.

2. Heat the broth to a lively simmer in a medium saucepan over medium-high heat.

3. Slowly pour egg mixture into the simmering broth. Stir constantly for a minute until the eggs form strips and flakes. Turn off heat.

4. Serve hot, topped with extra grated Parmesan.

PAIR WITH: Sesame-Cheese Bread Sticks (page 84)

Italian Mixed Green Salad with Parmigiano Vinaigrette

SERVES: 4 to 6 | **PREP TIME:** 15 minutes

Italian salad greens tend to have a bitter taste, but it's that bracing flavor that makes the salad exciting. In this recipe, the bitterness of escarole, radicchio, and dandelion is tempered by the calming presence of romaine lettuce and the creamy touch of Parmigiano vinaigrette.

1 head escarole, rinsed and patted dry

1 bunch dandelion greens, rinsed and patted dry

1 romaine lettuce heart, rinsed and patted dry

½ small head radicchio, rinsed and patted dry

⅓ cup extra-virgin olive oil

2 tablespoons mild vinegar (such as white wine vinegar or red wine vinegar)

¼ cup grated Parmesan cheese

Salt

Freshly ground black pepper

1. Remove the outer dark green leaves from the escarole. Cut off the core. Cut the inner pale green and white leaves into bite-size pieces (save darker leaves for sautéing or adding to soup). Cut the dandelion greens across the leaves, into small pieces. Slice the romaine into bite-size strips. Cut across the radicchio leaves to make thin strips.

2. Toss the cut salad greens together in a large salad bowl.

3. In a small mixing bowl, combine the olive oil, vinegar, and grated Parmesan. Stir briskly with a small spoon. Season with salt and pepper to taste. Drizzle dressing over salad and toss to coat.

INGREDIENT TIP: If you have trouble finding one or more of these greens, don't worry. Use the ones you can find. Any combination of two or more of these greens will make a great salad.

PAIR WITH: Roasted Cod with Crispy Parmigiano Crumbs (page 114)

Sicilian Orange and Fennel Salad

SERVES: 4 to 6 | **PREP TIME:** 15 minutes

Oranges grow in Sicily, and so does wild fennel. When my grandfather came from Sicily to the United States in 1912, he brought with him a sack of oranges to eat during his three-month voyage. By the time he arrived in New York, he never wanted to see an orange again! This salad always reminds me of my grandfather, and of the Sicilian flavors I imagine he grew up enjoying as a young boy.

2 navel oranges

1 bulb fennel

½ red onion

2 sprigs fresh mint leaves, finely chopped

Extra-virgin olive oil, for drizzling

Juice from 1 lemon

1 teaspoon honey

Salt

1. Peel the oranges. Cut them into ½-inch slices, across the segment grain. Then quarter each slice. Remove any seeds.

2. Trim off the long stems from the fennel bulb. Trim the root end. Cut off the tough outer layer. Cut remaining fennel bulb lengthwise in quarters. Cut each quarter lengthwise into very thin slices. Cut the red onion into thin, half-moon slices.

3. Combine the oranges, fennel, onion, and mint in a large serving bowl. Drizzle a little olive oil to coat. In a small bowl, mix together the lemon juice and honey. Drizzle this dressing over the salad and season with salt to taste. Toss well and serve.

INGREDIENT TIP: You can usually find fennel in the supermarkets. It's a white bulb with long green stems and feathery fronds.

PAIR WITH: Shrimp Scampi (page 119)

Panzanella Salad with Cucumbers

SERVES: 4 to 6 | **PREP TIME:** 15 minutes

Panzanella Salad turns a seemingly uninteresting ingredient (stale, day-old bread) into a main ingredient. The bread softens a bit in this recipe as it absorbs the juices of the tomatoes, olive oil, and vinegar. Fresh herbs round out the flavors. If you only have fresh bread on hand, tear it into bite-size pieces, spread it on a baking sheet, drizzle it with a little olive oil, season with salt and pepper, then bake at 375°F for 5 to 7 minutes, until dried and golden.

2 cucumbers

3 or 4 sprigs mint, leaves removed, stems discarded

3 or 4 large, ripe tomatoes, cut into thin wedges

1 small red onion, cut into thin half-moons

1 loaf day-old (slightly stale) Italian bread, torn into bite-size pieces

⅓ cup olive oil

⅓ cup vinegar

Salt

Freshly ground black pepper

1. Trim the cucumber ends, and slice cucumbers in half lengthwise. Then cut in thick half-moons. Tear mint leaves into small pieces. Toss cucumbers, mint, tomatoes, onion, and bread together in a large mixing bowl.

2. Dress with ⅓ cup each olive oil and vinegar. Season with salt and pepper to taste. Let salad sit for 15 to 30 minutes so the bread can absorb the juices and soften a bit before serving.

INGREDIENT TIP: The perfect time to make this salad is during summer, when the best tomatoes are available. When selecting tomatoes, choose ones that are deep red and as ripe as possible.

PAIR WITH: Pan-Roasted Chicken with Onion Pilaf (page 103)

Chopped Caprese Salad with Balsamic Vinegar

SERVES: 4 to 6 | **PREP TIME:** 15 minutes

The name *caprese* refers to Capri: that tiny, tall, beautiful island surrounded by the shimmering sea of the Amalfi Coast, in the region of Campania. To get the true essence of Capri in this salad, seek out the freshest ingredients possible. Unlike more traditional recipes, here I call for balsamic vinegar, which offers a nice new flavor, and I mix everything up in a bowl instead of laying out slices on a platter.

3 or 4 ripe tomatoes, cut into bite-size chunks

1½ cups small mozzarella balls (*bocconcini*), halved

1 shallot, peeled and minced

3 or 4 sprigs fresh basil leaves, torn into bite-size pieces

3 or 4 sprigs fresh mint leaves, torn into bite-size pieces

1 teaspoon dried oregano

¼ cup olive oil

3 tablespoons balsamic vinegar

Salt

Freshly ground black pepper

1. In a medium mixing bowl, combine the tomatoes, mozzarella, shallot, basil, mint, and oregano. Toss well.

2. Drizzle with the olive oil and balsamic vinegar, season with salt and pepper, and toss to coat. Serve.

INGREDIENT TIP: If you can't find the *bocconcini*, cut up a larger, fresh mozzarella ball into bite-size pieces.

PAIR WITH: Steamed Mussels with Cannellini Beans and Bacon (page 122)

Arugula-Radicchio Salad with Pears and Gorgonzola

SERVES: 4 to 6 | **PREP TIME:** 20 minutes

Pear, walnuts, and Gorgonzola go perfectly together. Add this trio of flavors to peppery baby arugula and assertive radicchio, and you've got a winning combination. For even more varied texture, I've included some dried cherries, which add a surprising pop of sweetness.

1 Bosc or Bartlett pear

Juice from 1 large lemon

2 or 3 scallions, green parts only

2 or 3 cups baby arugula

1 cup radicchio leaves, torn into bite-size pieces

⅓ cup dried cherries

⅓ cup walnuts, rough chopped

½ cup crumbled Gorgonzola

Extra-virgin olive oil, for drizzling

2 to 3 teaspoons mild vinegar (such as white wine vinegar)

Salt

1. Peel the pear, cut in half lengthwise, then cut in quarters lengthwise. Gently carve out the core and seeds. Cut pear into thin, bite-size slices. Toss pear with lemon juice to keep it from browning and for added flavor.

2. Cut scallions into small, thin circles.

3. In a large salad bowl, toss together the arugula, radicchio, pears (with lemon juice), scallions, dried cherries, walnuts, and Gorgonzola.

4. Drizzle the salad with a little olive oil and the vinegar, and toss well to coat the salad with the dressing. Season with salt to taste. Toss again and serve.

INGREDIENT TIP: Pears, even though they are a sweet fruit, love to appear in savory recipes. My favorite for this salad is Bosc pear. However, Bartlett and Anjou pears are equally delicious.

PAIR WITH: Fusilli with Red Wine and Pancetta (page 57)

Caesar Salad with Garlic-Anchovy Dressing

SERVES: 4 to 6 | **PREP TIME:** 15 minutes | **COOK TIME:** 6 minutes

Romaine is the traditional lettuce in Caesar Salad. It has great crunch because of its strong ribs, and its sweet flavor is a welcome contrast to the anchovy-based salad dressing. The salad, with its unusual combination of salty anchovy and grated Parmesan, was created in the 1920s by an Italian-born immigrant to Mexico, Caesar Cardini.

1 small baguette, cut into bite-size pieces

⅓ cup olive oil, plus more for drizzling

Salt

Freshly ground black pepper

1 large head romaine lettuce, or 2 romaine hearts, rinsed and patted dry

4 or 5 anchovy fillets, mashed

2 garlic cloves, peeled and grated

¼ cup freshly squeezed lemon juice (1–2 lemons)

1 tablespoon Worcestershire sauce

1 teaspoon Dijon mustard

3 tablespoons grated Parmesan

1. Preheat the oven to 375°F.

2. Toss the baguette pieces with a drizzling of olive oil to lightly coat. Season with salt and pepper. Spread out on a sheet pan in one layer. Bake until golden and crunchy, about 6 minutes. Set aside.

3. Cut the romaine in half lengthwise from the core to the leafy edges. Cut each half lengthwise again. Cut across the quarters to create bite-size pieces. Place the lettuce in a large salad bowl for serving.

4. In a medium mixing bowl, whisk together the mashed anchovies, garlic, olive oil, lemon juice, Worcestershire sauce, mustard, and Parmesan. Season with salt to taste. Pour the dressing over the lettuce. Add the croutons, toss well to coat, and serve.

VARIATION TIP: You can replace anchovy fillets with 2 teaspoons anchovy paste. It cuts the anchovy flavor by almost half, but it's easier and quicker to use. Some eaters may appreciate a lighter anchovy taste.

PAIR WITH: Chicken Saltimbocca with Sage and Prosciutto (page 102)

Red and Green Pepper Frittata, page 42

4

Polenta, Risottos, and Frittatas

Polenta, risotto, and frittatas are the ultimate Italian "blank canvases," perfect for showcasing all sorts of traditional and inventive flavors and ingredients. Polenta is a creamy, savory porridge made from cornmeal cooked with water and milk. When it cools, it hardens into a dense cake that you can fry and dress up, as in Sautéed Polenta Squares with Shaved Parmigiano (page 41). Risotto is an elegant dish made by following a very specific, yet simple, method: Italian rice is cooked slowly with broth, creating a rich, satisfying first course or side. Both polenta and risotto are more popular in the north of Italy than in the south, but frittatas are popular countrywide. A frittata, basically an Italian omelet, can be made with almost anything; it can include any combination of vegetables, herbs, cured meats, and/or pasta (see Spaghetti Cupcake Frittatas on page 43).

Soft and Cheesy Polenta with Roasted Mushrooms

SERVES: 4 to 6 | **PREP TIME:** 10 minutes | **COOK TIME:** 25 minutes

One of the stand-out flavors of this dish is Gorgonzola, Italy's super-savory blue cheese. When you stir the cheese into the polenta, it melts and becomes one with the cornmeal, creating an irresistible taste and consistency. Warm, soft polenta is so comforting and satisfying, and topping it with roasted thyme-infused mushrooms gives you a great contrast.

FOR THE MUSHROOMS

5 tablespoons extra-virgin olive oil, divided

1 shallot, peeled and thinly sliced

1 pound white mushrooms, trimmed and sliced

3 to 4 sprigs fresh thyme

FOR THE POLENTA

2 cups milk

3 cups water

1 cup cornmeal

2 tablespoons unsalted butter

½ cup crumbled Gorgonzola

½ cup grated Parmesan

¼ teaspoon ground nutmeg (optional)

Salt

Freshly ground black pepper

TO MAKE THE MUSHROOMS

1. Preheat the oven to 375°F.

2. Line a sheet pan with foil. Lightly oil the pan with about 2 tablespoons of olive oil. Toss sliced mushrooms and sliced shallot with 2 more tablespoons of oil. Spread out in one layer in the pan. Sprinkle thyme sprigs on top. Roast for about 15 minutes, until mushrooms are slightly wilted. Discard thyme.

TO MAKE THE POLENTA

1. While the mushrooms roast, bring the milk and water to a simmer. Sprinkle in the cornmeal, whisking the whole time. Cook on medium heat, stirring with a wooden spoon almost constantly, until the polenta thickens, about 20 minutes. Add the butter, cheeses, and nutmeg (if using), and season with salt and pepper. Polenta should be the consistency of a thick batter and pull away from the sides of the pan when done. Serve hot. Polenta thickens when cooled.

2. Spoon soft, hot polenta into individual serving bowls. Top with a spoonful or two of mushrooms.

VARIATION TIP: This dish can almost be whatever you like. Switch out the cheeses for your favorite flavors—just be sure to grate or shred the cheese first. Same for the mushrooms: feel free to swap them out for roasted peppers, wilted spinach, or steamed asparagus.

PAIR WITH: Chicken Saltimbocca with Sage and Prosciutto (page 102)

Sautéed Polenta Squares with Shaved Parmigiano

SERVES: 4 to 6 | **PREP TIME:** 5 minutes | **COOK TIME:** 40 minutes

When soft polenta cools, it solidifies into a tender, cake-like consistency that is perfect for slicing and topping with savory ingredients. Serve these fried polenta squares as an appetizer or side dish, or even as a snack.

½ cup water

2 cups milk

½ cup cornmeal

2 tablespoons unsalted butter, plus more for greasing the pan

Salt

2 tablespoons extra-virgin olive oil

½ cup shaved Parmesan or pecorino

1. Bring the water and milk to a simmer. Sprinkle in the cornmeal, whisking the whole time. Return the mixture to a simmer, whisking until it begins to thicken, then switch to a wooden spoon. Continue to stir, cooking until polenta is very thick, about 15 minutes. Stir in the butter, and salt to taste. Take off of the heat.

2. Butter a 9-by-13-inch pan, or quarter-sheet pan. Spread polenta into pan. Smooth it out to make an even, thin layer. Place pan in the refrigerator to set, about 15 minutes.

3. When the refrigerated polenta sets, cut it into about 2-inch squares or triangles. Heat 2 tablespoons of oil in a medium frying pan. When hot, add the cut polenta and fry until golden on both sides. Remove to a paper-towel-lined plate to drain, then blot.

4. Serve hot or room-temperature polenta squares/triangles topped with shaved Parmesan or pecorino cheese.

TIME-SAVING TIP: You can make and chill polenta a day or two ahead, then fry pieces when you're ready to serve. For best results, blot the polenta with paper towels before frying to remove any extra moisture.

PAIR WITH: Rice Salad with Chopped Vegetables and Roasted Peppers (page 50)

Red and Green Pepper Frittata

SERVES: 4 to 6 | **PREP TIME:** 10 minutes | **COOK TIME:** 12 minutes

I love mixing bell pepper colors. Green peppers have a much more assertive taste than their mild, red-pepper friends. The two together create a balance in taste that's very complementary (and pretty, too). In Italy, the word for bell peppers is *peperoni*—which can be confusing for tourists when they're ordering pizza.

1 small red bell pepper

1 small green bell pepper

3 to 4 tablespoons extra-virgin olive oil

Salt

Freshly ground black pepper

4 large eggs

1. Preheat the oven broiler.

2. Cut peppers in half. Pull off the stems and clean the inside of white membrane and seeds. Slice peppers into ½-inch strips.

3. Heat the olive oil in a medium stainless or cast iron sauté pan—the pan needs to go in the oven (make sure the handle is metal, too). When oil is hot, add the peppers. Sauté for 4 to 5 minutes on medium-high heat until peppers have softened, but still a little firm. Season with salt and pepper.

4. In a medium mixing bowl, whisk the eggs with a fork. Season with salt and pepper. Make sure there is at least a thin layer of oil still in the pan (or add a little). Pour the eggs over the peppers. Level the peppers with the eggs, using a spatula or fork, until the ingredients cover the pan evenly.

5. Lower heat to medium and let cook until the bottom is set, 2 to 3 minutes. Place the skillet in oven under broiler for 3 to 4 minutes until golden on top. IMPORTANT: remember to use a pot holder when taking out the skillet. It's easy to forget you have an oven-hot skillet and may just grab the handle as if it were on the stove. Once out, I keep a pot holder resting on the handle to remind me it's hot.

6. Loosen frittata from pan, and slide onto a dinner-size plate. Cut in wedges like a pizza. Serve warm or at room temperature.

PAIR WITH: Italian Mixed Green Salad with Parmigiano Vinaigrette (page 32)

Spaghetti Cupcake Frittatas

SERVES: 4 to 6 | **PREP TIME:** 20 minutes | **COOK TIME:** 20 minutes

When I lived in Rome, my Roman roommate, Enrica, showed me how to make a spaghetti frittata. At first, I was dubious. Pasta with eggs? In a frying pan? But after that first taste I was hooked. It's now my favorite type of frittata. These mini spaghetti frittatas are my version of Enrica's recipe. They are perfect for brunch, picnics, and after-work/after-school snacks.

1½ teaspoons salt, divided

½ pound spaghetti, strands broken into thirds

5 tablespoons unsalted butter, divided

½ teaspoon freshly ground black pepper

⅓ cup grated Parmesan or pecorino

3 eggs, lightly beaten

1 medium Roma (plum) tomato, cut into ¼-inch pieces

1. Preheat the oven to 400°F.

2. Bring 4 quarts of water to a boil in a pasta pot or large saucepan. When boiling, add a tablespoon of salt and then add spaghetti. Cook the spaghetti to al dente. Drain it and put it in a medium mixing bowl.

3. Cut 4 tablespoons of butter into pats and add to spaghetti. Stir to coat. Sprinkle in ½ teaspoon each salt and black pepper, and ¼ cup grated cheese. Stir to combine and coat spaghetti well. Add a little pasta water to moisten if too thick. Let pasta cool for about 5 minutes.

4. Butter a medium-size cupcake pan (should have 12 cups) with remaining butter.

5. Add the eggs to spaghetti mixture, and mix to combine well. Using a pair of tongs, lift a "tong-full" of pasta and place in a cupcake pan cup, just to the top. Fill all the cups with pasta. Sprinkle chopped tomato on top of each cup.

6. Bake for about 20 minutes until the tops look slightly golden, with some strands getting darker golden. Remove, let cool for about 5 minutes. Use a knife to loosen mini-frittatas around the edges. Lift out each one. Serve warm or at room temperature.

TIME-SAVING TIP: To save time, save this recipe for when you have leftover spaghetti. Any sauce will do. You can even make "cupcakes" with penne pasta or other small pasta shapes.

PAIR WITH: Butter-Braised Spinach with Slivered Almonds (page 95)

Sheet-Pan Frittata with Sun-Dried Tomatoes

SERVES: 4 to 6 | **PREP TIME:** 15 minutes | **COOK TIME:** 20 minutes

I love cutting this large frittata into small squares for an antipasto platter. The sun-dried tomato is nice and pungent, a perfect foil for the egg. Please note: moving the sheet pan with the liquid egg can be a bit tricky. Just carry it slowly, and place it on the oven rack that's easiest to reach.

5 large eggs

½ cup sun-dried tomatoes, diced (see Ingredient Tip)

⅓ cup grated Parmesan

Leaves from 1 to 2 sprigs fresh mint, minced

Salt

Freshly ground black pepper

1 tablespoon unsalted butter

1. Preheat the oven to 375°F.

2. In a medium mixing bowl, whisk together the eggs, sun-dried tomatoes, grated Parmesan, and mint. Season with salt and pepper.

3. Butter a 9-by-13-inch pan, or quarter sheet pan with at least 1-inch sides. Pour egg mixture into the pan. Gently slide into oven.

4. Bake for about 20 minutes until the egg solidifies and turns slightly golden.

5. Remove the pan from oven. Let cool for about 5 minutes. Cut frittata into 1- to 2-inch squares, either in the pan or turned out onto a cutting board. Serve warm or at room temperature.

INGREDIENT TIP: I prefer to buy unmarinated sun-dried tomatoes. You can usually find them in packets, uncoated and totally dry. These tend to have the cleanest flavor.

PAIR WITH: Chopped Caprese Salad with Balsamic Vinegar (page 35)

Risi e Bisi (Venetian Rice and Peas)

SERVES: 4 to 6 | **PREP TIME:** 10 minutes | **COOK TIME:** 20 minutes

This homey Venetian classic couldn't be humbler. It's just rice and peas. The dish is cooked risotto style, which means you actively stir in the warm broth little by little until the rice is cooked. What makes Risi e Bisi different from risotto is that, at the end of cooking, you add extra broth to make it soupy.

4 cups low-sodium vegetable or chicken broth

5 tablespoons unsalted butter, divided

1 tablespoon extra-virgin olive oil

1 medium onion, minced

1 cup arborio or other short-grain rice

¼ cup white wine

2 cups frozen peas, thawed

Leaves from 2 to 3 fresh Italian parsley sprigs, minced

⅓ cup grated Parmesan

1. Heat the broth in a medium saucepan until warmed.

2. In a heavy-bottomed saucepan or sauté pan with 2-inch sides, melt 2 tablespoons of butter and 1 tablespoon of olive oil. Add the minced onion and sauté until softened but not colored.

3. Add the rice and stir until rice is coated with oil and butter and heated until hot. Add the wine. The pan will sizzle with steam. Allow wine to evaporate, stirring to prevent the rice from sticking.

4. Start adding the warmed broth to the pan, about a cup at a time, stirring until it begins to evaporate. Continue adding broth little by little, until the rice becomes al dente.

5. Just before the rice is done, add the peas and parsley. Stir to incorporate. When the rice is cooked, add enough broth to keep it a little soupy. Stir in the last tablespoon of butter and the grated Parmesan. Serve hot.

PAIR WITH: Tilapia Poached in Savory Tomato-Tarragon Sauce (page 117)

Lemony Risotto with Asparagus

SERVES: 4 to 6 | **PREP TIME:** 10 minutes | **COOK TIME:** 20 minutes

Risotto is a style of cooking rice that creates a creamy, elegant result. It requires constant stirring while the rice absorbs the broth and eventually becomes al dente—cooked through but still firm to the bite. There are countless ingredients you can add to risotto, but the basic recipe always remains the same. In this one we add lemon zest and asparagus. Note: There's a saying that you should always stir risotto in the same direction. That's what I do (keeping with tradition), but I'm not sure if it really matters.

4 cups low-sodium vegetable or chicken broth

12 asparagus spears

4 tablespoons unsalted butter, divided

1 tablespoon extra-virgin olive oil

1 medium onion, minced

1 cup arborio rice

½ cup dry white wine

Salt

Zest from 2 small lemons

½ cup grated Parmesan

1. Heat the broth in a medium pot until warmed. Keep on a low-heat burner throughout the cooking.

2. Cut off the woody ends of the asparagus. Then cut the asparagus into bite-size pieces. Reserve.

3. In a heavy-bottomed saucepan or sauté pan with at least 2-inch sides, melt 2 tablespoons of butter and one tablespoon of olive oil. When hot, add the onion and sauté until softened but not colored. Add the rice and stir until the rice is coated with oil and butter and heated until hot. Add the wine. The pan will sizzle with steam. Allow wine to evaporate, stirring to prevent the rice from sticking.

4. Start adding broth to the pan, about 1 cup at a time—the amount should come to ½ inch above the rice level. Continue to stir until broth begins to evaporate. The pan should be simmering on medium to medium-high heat. Then add more broth little by little, continuing to stir until the rice becomes al dente, 12 to 15 minutes.

5. About three-quarters of the way through cooking, add the cut asparagus. Season rice with a little salt.

6. When al dente, add 2 tablespoons of butter, the lemon zest, and the cheese. Stir to combine. The consistency should be creamy and still very moist. Adjust seasoning with salt if necessary. Serve immediately.

INGREDIENT TIPS: Arborio rice is easy to find in most grocery stores, and it will really give you the best results. If you start to run out of broth near the end of cooking, it's okay to use water instead.

PAIR WITH: Shrimp Scampi (page 119)

CUCINA POVERA

The Italian term *cucina povera* translates to "peasant cooking" in English. When meat, fish, or other expensive ingredients are scarce in the kitchen, invention is necessary. Stale bread suddenly becomes an important ingredient, as in the bread and tomato soup Pappa al Pomodoro on page 30, or it's used to make bread crumbs for stuffing. Humble ingredients, like cornmeal, rice, and eggs, shine with the right flavors and just a few added ingredients (see Sheet-Pan Frittata with Sun-Dried Tomatoes, page 44; Soft and Cheesy Polenta with Roasted Mushrooms, page 40; and Baked Rice with Peas and Celery, page 49). *Cucina povera* is a cuisine that shows us what we don't need, inviting us to invent delicious new recipes with the most basic of ingredients.

Risotto Milanese with Saffron

SERVES: 4 to 6 | **PREP TIME:** 10 minutes | **COOK TIME:** 20 minutes

Risotto Milanese is a classic dish from the region of Lombardia. In this recipe, rice is cooked in the typical risotto style, with the only added ingredient being saffron, which lends the cooked rice a yellow hue and deep flavor. Risotto Milanese is almost always paired with osso buco.

4 cups low-sodium vegetable broth (for vegetarians) or chicken broth

4 tablespoons unsalted butter, divided

1 tablespoon extra-virgin olive oil

1 small onion, minced

1 cup arborio rice

⅓ cup dry white wine

½ teaspoon saffron threads

½ cup grated Parmesan cheese

Salt

1. Heat the broth in a medium pot until warmed. Keep warm on a low burner.

2. For the rice, use a medium, thick-bottomed saucepan or sauté pan with at least 2-inch sides. Melt 2 tablespoons of butter and 1 tablespoon of olive oil in the pan over medium heat. Add onion and sauté on medium-high until softened but not colored, about 3 minutes.

3. Add the rice and stir until the rice is coated with oil and butter and heated until hot. Add the wine. The pan will sizzle with steam. Allow wine to evaporate, stirring to prevent the rice from sticking.

4. Start adding broth to the pan, about 1 cup at a time—the amount should come to ½ inch above the rice. Continue to stir until broth begins to evaporate. The pan should be simmering on medium to medium-high heat. Then add more broth little by little, continuing to stir until the rice becomes al dente, 12 to 15 minutes.

5. About two-thirds of the way through cooking, place the saffron in a small bowl and add some of the hot broth. Let it steep about 3 minutes. Stir the saffron broth into the rice near the end.

6. When rice is al dente, add remaining 2 tablespoons of butter, and the cheese. Stir to combine. Season with salt to taste. Serve immediately.

TIME-SAVING TIP: Risotto needs to be served immediately, since it can get sticky as it sits. If you're cooking risotto for company, try this trick: Cook the rice, stirring and adding broth little by little, for 10 minutes, then turn off the heat. When company arrives, start up the cooking and stirring again. It'll take about another 5 minutes and will still have the perfect consistency at the end.

PAIR WITH: Veal Osso Buco Braised in Red Wine (page 108)

Baked Rice with Peas and Celery

SERVES: 4 to 6 | **PREP TIME:** 15 minutes | **COOK TIME:** 50 minutes

I grew up with this casserole-style dish. It's a little bit unusual, with some unfamiliar steps, but it's easy to make, and the resulting flavors are well worth the effort. My mom learned this recipe from our Sicilian upstairs neighbor in Brooklyn, whom I knew as Aunt Mary, a good friend who became my mother's cooking mentor. Though baked rice is not particularly Sicilian, it is an example of what Italian immigrants came up with as they acclimated to American culture.

Salt

1 cup long-grain rice

2 or 3 tablespoons
extra-virgin olive oil

8 to 10 ounces mushrooms,
rinsed or brushed clean,
roughly chopped

1 stalk celery, diced finely

1 onion, diced finely

1 egg

1 cup low-sodium vegetable
or chicken broth

1 cup frozen peas, thawed

Freshly ground
black pepper

2½ tablespoons
unsalted butter, plus
more for the pan

½ cup bread
crumbs, divided

1. Preheat the oven to 375°F.

2. In a medium saucepan bring 3 to 4 cups of water to a boil. Add some salt and the rice. Cook at a simmer for 12 to 15 minutes until tender. Drain. Set aside.

3. Meanwhile, heat olive oil in a medium skillet until hot. Add the mushrooms. Cook about 5 minutes until they are wilted and cooked through. Season with salt. Remove them from pan and set aside. Add a little more oil; heat till hot; add the celery and onion. Cook until softened, about 5 minutes. Season with salt. Remove from pan and add to the mushrooms.

4. In a large mixing bowl, beat the egg with the broth. Add the cooked rice, peas, and celery-mushroom-onion mixture. Combine well. Taste for seasoning and add salt if needed. Add some black pepper.

5. Using ½ tablespoon of butter, grease a medium casserole dish, and coat with all the bread crumbs except 2 tablespoons. Shake out excess crumbs. Pour in rice mixture and smooth top evenly. Sprinkle the rest of the bread crumbs on top. Cut remaining 2 tablespoons of butter into smaller pieces and dot the top with butter pieces. Bake for about 40 minutes until the top is golden. Let sit for 5 minutes or more before spooning out to serve.

TIME-SAVING TIP: This dish is even better the next day, so feel free to bake it the day before you need it. Keep it in the refrigerator, and reheat when you're ready.

PAIR WITH: Rustic Sausage Meatballs (page 105)

Rice Salad with Chopped Vegetables and Roasted Peppers

SERVES: 4 to 6 | **PREP TIME:** 15 minutes | **COOK TIME:** 15 minutes

Giardiniera is a popular Italian condiment—assorted vegetables pickled in vinegar and packed in a jar—which can be found in most grocery stores near the pickles and olives. These vinegary vegetables have an intense taste, but they are delicious paired with the neutral flavor of rice. Rice Salad with *giardiniera* is a northern Italian favorite. I add a few roasted red peppers, olives, and some fresh tomato to give this dish even more texture and balance.

5–6 cups water

Salt

2 cups long-grain rice

1 (16-ounce) jar Italian *giardiniera* (or other pickled vegetables)

1 cup pitted black or green olives, chopped

2 roasted red peppers (from a jar), cut into bite-size pieces

½ cup fresh grape tomatoes, quartered

Extra-virgin olive oil, for drizzling

Juice of 1 lemon

Freshly ground black pepper

1. In a large saucepan, bring 5 to 6 cups of water to a boil. Add some salt and the rice. Cook at a simmer for 12 to 15 minutes until tender. Drain. Add the rice to a large mixing bowl.

2. Meanwhile, drain the *giardinera* vegetables and chop them into bite-size pieces. Add to the rice. Add olives, peppers, and tomatoes. Season well with salt and pepper. Drizzle olive oil to coat all. Add lemon juice. Stir well to combine. Serve at room temperature, or cold.

TIME-SAVING TIP: Make this salad a few days before you need it, and nibble on a small bowlful every time you want a great snack or pick-me-up.

PAIR WITH: Baked Parchment Packets with Tilapia, Thyme, and Lemon (page 118)

Linguine with Fra Diavolo Shrimp Sauce, page 68

5

Pastas and Sauces

My dad used to tell me a story about his father coming home from work via the subway in Brooklyn: the train platform was so close to the back of my grandfather's house that, as soon as he got off the train, he would call out to my grandmother, "Put the water on for pasta!" He didn't want to wait for the water to boil, yet he knew that my grandmother was waiting to start the water, since pasta should always be eaten right after it finishes cooking (to prevent it from sticking together and losing its perfect texture). Later in my life, I learned the popular Italian saying, "pasta waits for no one," and it reminds me of my grandfather calling from the train.

Pasta is the soul food of Italian cuisine—at once comforting, delicious, nutritious, and easy to prepare. There already seems to be an infinite number of pasta recipes, and every time I go to Italy, I come home with two or three new ones. Each city, each town, and each household has their own way of seasoning, saucing, and cooking Italy's iconic, multi-shaped noodles. To get the best results, most of the recipes in this chapter can be made in the time it takes to boil your pasta. And in the true spirit of *cucina povera* (see page 47), even the pasta water is an ingredient in some recipes, such as Spaghetti Cacio e Pepe (page 62), and True Fettuccine Alfredo (page 63).

Fresh Egg Pasta Dough

SERVES: 4 to 6 | **PREP TIME:** 45 minutes | **COOK TIME:** 3 minutes

Fresh Egg Pasta Dough can be used for many different pasta shapes. It takes a little time, but it's worth trying at least once—so you can say you did. It's a fun thing to do with family and friends (and as a bonus, many hands will make the work go faster). We make fresh pasta in my cooking classes all the time, and everyone masters it quickly. Here's how to make fettuccine, which is delicious in True Fettuccine Alfredo (page 63) and Pasta with 15-Minute Tomato Sauce (page 58).

2 cups all-purpose flour

½ teaspoon salt

3 large eggs, lightly beaten

2 teaspoons extra-virgin olive oil

1. Whisk the flour and salt in a large mixing bowl. Create a well in the middle. Mix the eggs with the olive oil and pour egg mixture into the well center. Using a fork, slowly mix the flour into the egg, until the dough starts to comes together. If you get a nice ball of dough and there's still some flour left in the bowl, don't feel compelled to include it all. Gather the dough and knead on a clean work surface until most of the floury color disappears. Shape into a ball and cover with plastic wrap. Let rest for about 30 minutes at room temperature (if possible), or use right away.

2. *Without a pasta machine:* Cut the ball into 4 quarters. Work with one quarter at a time, wrapping the rest of the dough in plastic to keep from drying out. On a clean work surface, lightly dusted with flour, roll out a quarter of the dough as thin as possible, about ⅛-inch. For fettuccine, using a knife, or a wheel cutter, make strips of pasta about ¼ inch wide. Or gently fold pasta sheet into 2 or 3 folds. Cut into ¼-inch strips and shake out pieces. Lay out strips on a lightly floured sheet pan. Repeat with rest of dough. (Note: for shorter strands, you can cut your dough sheet in half before making the fettuccine strips.)

3. *If you have a pasta machine:* Cut the dough into quarters. Work with one quarter at a time, keeping the rest of the dough covered in plastic. Flatten the dough quarter. Set the pasta machine at the widest setting (usually the lowest number). Pass the dough through the machine. Fold it in thirds and pass it through the first setting again. Then roll the dough through, advancing the numbers one by one, until you reach the number before the last, or the desired thickness. Cut the stretched dough into 2 or 3 lengths, depending on how long you want the fettuccine. Use the cutter for fettuccine on the machine and pass the dough pieces through, separating the strands when done.

4. Bring about 4 quarts of water to a boil in a pasta pot or large saucepan. Add 1 tablespoon salt, then the pasta. Cook, stirring to keep stands separate, till al dente, about 3 minutes. Drain. Add sauce, and serve.

VARIATION TIP: For spinach pasta, add ¼ cup of minced fresh spinach to the egg mixture, and increase the amount of flour by ½ cup.

PAIR WITH: Roasted Asparagus with Shallot and Parmigiano (page 89)

‖‖‖ ‖‖‖‖‖‖‖‖‖‖‖ ‖‖‖‖‖‖‖‖‖‖‖ ‖‖‖‖‖‖‖‖‖‖‖‖‖‖‖‖‖‖‖‖‖‖‖‖‖‖‖‖‖‖‖‖‖‖‖‖ ‖‖‖‖‖‖‖‖‖‖‖ ‖‖‖‖‖‖‖‖‖‖‖ ‖‖‖‖‖‖‖

HOW TO COOK PASTA

Follow these simple instructions to cook any dried pasta to perfection:

1. Bring a large pot of water to a rolling boil. When the water boils, add enough salt to make it as salty as the ocean (about a tablespoon or more).
2. Add the pasta and stir well to prevent it from sticking together.
3. Once the water comes back to a boil, set a timer for the time specified on the pasta's packaging for al dente—usually 8 to 10 minutes. Thicker-cut pasta will need more time to cook, and thin pasta like capellini will need less time. Do not add oil to the water. Oil coats the pasta, preventing any sauce you use from sticking to the pasta and adding an extra flavor that might not go well with the rest of your recipe.
4. How do you know it's done? There's only one way: taste it. Pasta should be cooked *al dente*, or "to the tooth," which means cooked through but still firm.

For fresh-made pasta, it's a little different: Add it to the salted boiling water and cook for no more than 3 or 4 minutes. Any longer, and the fresh pasta can turn to mush.

‖‖‖ ‖‖‖‖‖‖‖‖‖‖‖ ‖‖‖‖‖‖‖‖‖‖‖ ‖‖‖‖‖‖‖‖‖‖‖‖‖‖‖‖‖‖‖‖‖‖‖‖‖‖‖‖‖‖‖‖‖‖‖‖ ‖‖‖‖‖‖‖‖‖‖‖ ‖‖‖‖‖‖‖‖‖‖‖ ‖‖‖‖‖‖‖

Fresh Eggless Pasta Dough

SERVES: 4 to 6 | **PREP TIME:** 15 minutes, plus 30 minutes for dough to rest | **COOK TIME:** 3 minutes

In all my travels to Italy, I have encountered eggless pasta dough most frequently in the southern regions. The recipe requires only three ingredients: flour, water, and salt. In Sicily, they sometimes use semolina flour. In Puglia, we once used whole-wheat flour with water. But all-purpose flour, the flour most easily found in stores, is a great choice. Here is a recipe for eggless pasta dough with a sample pasta shape for you to try: *trofie. Trofie* originated in the Italian Riviera in the region of Liguria; it's fun to make, and it holds sauce well.

FOR THE PASTA DOUGH

2 cups unbleached all-purpose flour, plus extra

1 tablespoon plus ¼ teaspoon salt, divided

⅔ cup water

TO MAKE THE PASTA DOUGH

1. Whisk the flour and salt in a large mixing bowl.

2. Make a well in the center. Pour ⅔ cup of water in the center and, using a fork, whisk the flour into the water until the dough starts to come together.

3. Gather the dough and knead it on a lightly floured surface. If it's too sticky, add a little flour; if it's too dry, add a little water. Knead for about 5 minutes until smooth; shape the dough into a ball, and cover with plastic wrap.

4. Let rest for 30 minutes at room temperature (if possible), or use right away.

TO MAKE THE *TROFIE* PASTA SHAPE

1. Break off a small handful of dough. Roll dough into a long rope about ½ inch thick. Cut rope into ½-inch pieces. Roll each piece with a swift motion between your palms until the dough becomes elongated and twisted. It should look like a thin, short piece of twisted rope. Repeat with the rest of the dough. Place the finished *trofie* on a floured sheet pan or surface.

2. Bring 4 quarts of water to a boil in a pasta pot or large saucepan. Add 1 tablespoon salt and the pasta. Stir occasionally to keep from clumping. Cook for about 3 minutes until pasta is al dente. Add your favorite sauce.

TECHNIQUE TIP: Try to keep the shaped pasta pieces as thin as possible. They will inflate a little when boiled.

USE IN: Pasta with 30-Minute Meat Sauce (page 59) or Farfalle with Grated Zucchini and Cream (page 66)

Fusilli with Red Wine and Pancetta

SERVES: 4 to 6 | **PREP TIME:** 10 minutes | **COOK TIME:** 15 minutes

I love using fusilli pasta here, because it most perfectly matches the pasta shape used when I first tasted this dish. My cooking group and I were enjoying a wine tasting in the Chianti classico region of Tuscany. While we sipped Chianti on the patio of the vineyard, we were served this pasta made by the lady of the house. The pasta is actually cooked in red wine, which gives the finished dish a beautiful color. Pancetta and sage round out the flavorings—earthy, Tuscan, and very much from a vineyard. You can also try either of the fresh pasta recipes (pages 54 and 56) to go with this sauce.

2 tablespoons extra-virgin olive oil

¼ pound pancetta, diced

Salt

1 pound cut pasta, such as fusilli or corkscrew shape

1 cup Chianti wine or favorite dry red wine

Freshly ground black pepper

½ cup grated Parmesan or pecorino or combination

8 to 10 fresh sage leaves, diced

1. In a pasta pot or large saucepan, bring 4 quarts of water to a boil.

2. Meanwhile, place the olive oil and chopped pancetta in a small frying pan. Cook until the pancetta is lightly browned, about 5 minutes. Remove from the heat and set aside.

3. Add 1 tablespoon salt to the boiling water, then stir in the pasta and cook until it is almost done, just before al dente (the pasta will cook some more in the wine).

4. Meanwhile, pour the wine into a large, deep sauté pan and bring it to a simmer over medium heat. Add a pinch of salt. When the pasta is almost done cooking, use a skimmer or strainer to scoop the pasta out of the pot, and drop it into the simmering wine. Let the pasta cook at a lively simmer, stirring frequently, for about 2 minutes or until the wine is mostly or completely absorbed. Season with salt and pepper.

5. Scrape the pancetta and its oil into the pan with the pasta, stir in the cheese and sage leaves, and season with salt and pepper to taste. Serve hot.

PAIR WITH: Easy Crab Cakes (page 123)

Pasta with 15-Minute Tomato Sauce

SERVES: 4 to 6 | **PREP TIME:** 5 minutes | **COOK TIME:** 15 minutes

You don't have to spend hours making a great tomato sauce. This quick marinara is my go-to recipe for a fast, authentic taste.

2 tablespoons extra-virgin olive oil

1 medium onion, finely diced

¼ cup dry white wine

1 (28-ounce) can crushed tomatoes

Salt

Freshly ground black pepper

1 pound pasta (or pasta from fresh pasta recipes, pages 54 and 56)

1. Heat 4 quarts of water in a pasta pot or large saucepan.

2. Heat oil in a medium saucepan. When hot, add onion. Cook on medium to medium-high heat for about 3 to 5 minutes until onion has softened.

3. Add the wine. Let the wine evaporate to about half its volume.

4. Add tomatoes. Season lightly with salt and pepper. Let simmer for 10 to 15 minutes.

5. When pasta water is boiling, add 1 tablespoon salt. Add pasta. Cook to al dente. Drain.

6. Add pasta to a large serving bowl. Coat with tomato sauce.

INGREDIENT TIP: If you like garlic, add a peeled garlic clove when sautéing the onion. And remember: Italians like some sauce with their pasta—not some pasta with their sauce. Avoid drowning the pasta in sauce when you serve it.

PAIR WITH: Broiled Lamb Chops with Salsa Verde (page 111)

Pasta with 30-Minute Meat Sauce

SERVES: 4 to 5 | **PREP TIME:** 10 minutes | **COOK TIME:** 30 minutes

Yes, there are meat sauces that take hours to cook; that's when you're using cuts of meat that need low-and-slow braises to break down and get tender. For a quicker version, I like to use ground beef, which cooks in minutes and adds the perfect amount of meatiness to the sauce in much less time.

2 tablespoons extra-virgin olive oil

1 medium onion, finely diced

2 garlic cloves, peeled and smashed

½ pound ground beef

⅓ cup dry white wine

1 (28-ounce) can crushed tomatoes

Salt

Freshly ground black pepper

1 pound pasta (or pasta from fresh pasta recipes, pages 54 and 56)

½ cup grated Parmesan for servings

1. Heat oil in a medium saucepan. Add onion and garlic. Cook on medium heat until onion softens, about 3 to 4 minutes.

2. Add beef. Brown meat, breaking up into smaller pieces, leaving some larger chunks (making for a rustic mixture of meat pieces). When the meat is no longer pink, add the wine. Let it sizzle and mostly evaporate.

3. Add the can of tomatoes. Season with salt and pepper. Stir to combine. Simmer for 20 minutes, cover askew.

4. Heat 4 quarts of water in a pasta pot or large saucepan. When boiling, salt the water. Add the pasta. Cook until al dente. When done, drain. Add to a large serving bowl. Spoon on some sauce and gently coat. You can add extra sauce on top of individual servings, and pass around grated Parmesan.

VARIATION TIP: For variety, layer this sauce with cooked, cut pasta in a casserole dish. Add chunks of mozzarella and bake until bubbly.

PAIR WITH: Asparagus Wrapped in Prosciutto with Crispy Bread Crumbs (page 90)

Spaghetti with Spicy Aglio e Olio

SERVES: 4 to 6 | **PREP TIME:** 5 minutes | **COOK TIME:** 15 minutes

This recipe is the king of *La Spaghettata di Mezzanotte*—quick spaghetti dishes you make for friends at midnight. Sometimes after an evening on the town, you invite everyone to your place and take ten minutes to create a very tasty pasta. I've done this in New York City, dragging everyone up four flights of stairs to my small studio apartment. *Aglio* is garlic. *Olio* is oil. It's pretty much all you need.

Salt

1 pound spaghetti

⅓ cup extra-virgin olive oil

3 garlic cloves, peeled and thinly sliced

2 teaspoons crushed red pepper flakes, or to taste

Leaves from 4 sprigs fresh Italian parsley, roughly chopped

Freshly ground black pepper

1. Heat 4 quarts of water in a pasta pot or large saucepan. Bring to a boil. Add 1 tablespoon of salt. Add the spaghetti. Cook until al dente. Reserve ¾ cup of pasta water. Drain the pasta.

2. Meanwhile, add the oil, garlic, and red pepper flakes to a large sauté pan. Heat until garlic is just turning golden.

3. Add the drained pasta to the oil and garlic, then cook on medium-low heat, tossing pasta in oil. Add the parsley. Season with salt and pepper. Add some pasta water to keep the pasta moist and to help coat the strands with the oil. When the pasta looks shiny, it's done. Serve hot.

TIME-SAVING TIP: For quick pasta dishes like this one, always start by putting the water on to boil. It's the step that will take the longest.

PAIR WITH: Roasted Salmon with Olives, Capers, and Herbs (page 116)

Spaghetti alla Carbonara

SERVES: 4 to 6 | **PREP TIME:** 10 minutes | **COOK TIME:** 10 minutes

Spaghetti alla Carbonara is probably the most iconic pasta dish of Rome. I learned it from a Roman when I did an undergraduate year in Rome. Romans are very particular about the ingredients. They insist you use guanciale, cured pig's jowl (not pancetta), and pecorino cheese (not Parmigiano-Reggiano). The reason is taste, of course, but for years I made it with pancetta and Parmesan, and the dish was just as lovely. This is one of those pasta dishes in which the cook time is only as long as it takes for the spaghetti to boil.

Salt

1 pound dried spaghetti

¼ pound guanciale, diced (or pancetta)

1 tablespoon extra-virgin olive oil

4 large eggs

1 or 2 cups grated pecorino cheese or more as needed, plus extra for serving

2 teaspoons freshly ground black pepper

1. Bring 4 quarts of water to a boil in a pasta pot or large saucepan. When boiling, add 1 tablespoon of salt, and add the spaghetti. While the pasta cooks, make the sauce.

2. In a small skillet, sauté the *guanciale* or pancetta in the tablespoon of oil until cooked through, about 4 minutes. Set aside.

3. In a large serving bowl, break the eggs, add the cheese and pepper, and salt to taste. Mix together thoroughly with a fork. Add more cheese if needed, to make a pasty (rather than thin and watery) mixture.

4. Just before the pasta is done, spoon out a cup of the pasta water and reserve. When pasta is al dente, drain it and immediately add it to the bowl containing the egg mixture. *Immediately*, mix the pasta and eggs together. I usually have a wooden spoon and fork at the ready, or a pair of tongs. Pull the pasta strands through the eggs over and over. The hot pasta will "cook" the egg, and the egg mixture will give the pasta a creamy coat of sauce. When you see the pasta has absorbed all the eggy mixture, add the pancetta in its oil, and mix thoroughly. Add a few spoonfuls of reserved pasta water if the dish is a little dry. Serve hot, passing around extra cheese.

TECHNIQUE TIP: It's essential to mix the hot pasta and the egg mixture as soon as the pasta lands in the bowl. Have your utensils ready at the sides of the bowl so you can begin tossing right away. I usually use a wooden spoon in one hand and a large wooden fork in the other hand.

PAIR WITH: Broccoli Rabe with Garlic and Hot Pepper (page 91)

Spaghetti Cacio e Pepe

SERVES: 4 to 6 | **PREP TIME:** 10 minutes | **COOK TIME:** 12 minutes

Cacio is the cheese; *pepe* is the black pepper. And that's about it for this classic Roman dish. Oh, yes, and then there's the butter—a whole stick. The first time I ate this in Rome, my friend Malena (who lives in Rome) led my cooking class group on a very long walk. We finally arrived in the neighborhood of Trastevere and to the acclaimed restaurant Roma Sparita. *Cacio e Pepe* is their claim to fame, and they serve it in bowls made of pecorino cheese. This is a pasta dish that's easy to make at home—another quick *spaghettata*.

Salt

1 pound spaghetti

1 stick (8 tablespoons) unsalted butter

3 tablespoons extra-virgin olive oil

1 tablespoon freshly ground black pepper, or more to taste

1 cup grated pecorino cheese

1. Heat 4 quarts of water in a pasta pot or large saucepan. Bring to a boil. Add 1 tablespoon of salt. Add the spaghetti. Cook to al dente. Reserve 1 cup pasta water before draining.

2. Meanwhile, in a large sauté pan, heat the butter, oil, and pepper until butter melts and sizzles a little. Season lightly with salt.

3. When pasta is done, drain it and add it to the sauté pan. Cook over medium heat, tossing pasta and coating it with the mixture. Add about ⅓ of the cheese, lightly sprinkling. Toss to coat. Add about half of the pasta water. Add more cheese, tossing a little at a time, until it is all used up. Add more pasta water if needed to moisten. Consistency should be a thick, moist coating on the pasta. Serve hot.

INGREDIENT TIP: If you like the assertive taste of pepper, try increasing the amount of black pepper to 2 tablespoons. Sprinkling the cheese little by little helps keep it from clumping up.

PAIR WITH: One-Pan Sausage and Peppers (page 104)

True Fettuccine Alfredo

SERVES: 4 to 6 | **PREP TIME:** 5 minutes | **COOK TIME:** 12 minutes

Here's a surprise: There's no cream in Fettuccine Alfredo. The creaminess is created by mixing together Parmesan cheese with butter and then pasta water, using lots of quick stirring and tossing. Pasta water contains salt and starch from the just-cooked pasta, which helps add flavor to the dish and creates a smooth sauce. This dish originated in Rome, where there's some quarrel over which "alfredo" restaurant created it. In Rome they simply call it pasta with butter.

1 tablespoon salt

1 pound fettuccine pasta (or use fresh egg pasta fettuccine, page 54)

2 sticks (½ pound) unsalted butter, at room temperature

2 to 2½ cups grated Parmesan

1. Fill a large pasta pot with 4 quarts of water and bring to a boil. Add 1 tablespoon salt. Add the fettuccine.

2. Meanwhile, slice the butter into thin pats and lay them out in one layer along the bottom of a large, shallow serving bowl. Butter should be room-temperature soft, but not melting.

3. Cook pasta until al dente. Before draining, reserve ¾ cup of the pasta water. Drain pasta.

4. Pour the drained pasta on top of the butter and sprinkle about one quarter of the cheese on top. Using a large fork and spoon, (or two forks), toss the pasta quickly, coating it with the butter and cheese. Add some of the pasta water—about half. Continue to toss. Add the rest of the cheese little by little, tossing and coating in between each addition.

5. Keep tossing until the pasta is coated in the creaminess of the butter-cheese-water combination. Add more water if mixture is too thick. Serve hot.

TECHNIQUE TIP: It's important to add the cheese little by little. If you add it all at once, it can clump up, and you won't get a creamy consistency.

PAIR WITH: Cod Acqua Pazza (page 115)

Amalfi Lemony Tuna Capellini

SERVES: 4 to 6 | **PREP TIME:** 15 minutes | **COOK TIME:** 8 minutes

Along the Amalfi Coast are small towns built into the cliffs by the sea. You can park yourself at one of their restaurants and have the sea glimmering in your eyes, with giant lemons hanging from the vine above you. This dish encapsulates the fresh atmosphere and briny lemony taste from Amalfi. The sauce requires nothing more than a bit of chopping, so by the time your pasta is done cooking, you'll be ready to serve the whole meal.

Salt

1 pound capellini pasta

1 (5-ounce) can tuna, preferably packed in olive oil

3 medium lemons, zested and juiced

2 garlic cloves, peeled and minced

Leaves from 5 to 6 sprigs fresh Italian parsley, minced

¼ cup extra-virgin olive oil, or more as needed

½ cup grated Parmesan, plus more for serving

Freshly ground black pepper

1. Heat 4 quarts of water in a pasta pot or large saucepan. Bring to a boil.

2. When water boils, add 1 tablespoon salt. Add the capellini. Cook to al dente.

3. Drain tuna and break it up into flakes. Put tuna in a large mixing bowl. Add lemon zest, lemon juice, garlic, parsley, ¼ cup olive oil, and grated Parmesan. Season to taste with salt and pepper. Mix all to combine.

4. When pasta is done, reserve ½ cup pasta water. Drain pasta. Add cooked capellini to lemon-tuna mixture. Toss to combine and coat. Add a little pasta water or olive oil to moisten if needed. Salt to taste.

5. Serve with extra grated cheese for individual servings.

VARIATION TIP: This recipe is also delicious without the tuna, so feel free to leave out the fish for a lemony vegetarian option.

PAIR WITH: Clams Oreganata (page 20)

Orecchiette with Cauliflower and Crispy Bread

SERVES: 4 to 6 | **PREP TIME:** 15 minutes | **COOK TIME:** 20 to 25 minutes

When I lived in Rome for a year as an undergrad student, my best friend, Malena, was the daughter of an American diplomat stationed in Rome. Malena and I remained friends for years. She stayed in Rome and married a Roman. Recently, when I went to Rome with a group of my cooking class students, Malena came to our apartment and demonstrated this classic Roman fall recipe. It's another one of those genius dishes that is very simple, yet incredibly tasty.

1 large head cauliflower

1 tablespoon salt, plus more to taste

1 loaf Italian peasant bread, or similar

½ cup extra-virgin olive oil, divided

3 garlic cloves, peeled and minced

1 pound orecchiette pasta, or other favorite short, cut pasta

½ cup grated pecorino or Parmesan cheese, plus more for serving

1. Preheat the oven to 375°F.

2. Heat 4 quarts of water in a pasta pot or large saucepan. Bring to a boil.

3. Cut the cauliflower in half. Cut out the bottom core and discard. Cut the rest of the cauliflower into 2-inch floweret pieces. When the water comes to a boil, add 1 tablespoon salt. Add cauliflower.

4. Meanwhile, tear up the Italian bread into bite-size pieces. Toss bread with about ¼ cup olive oil, then add the minced garlic. Spread out on a sheet pan and bake in a hot oven until golden and crispy, about 8 minutes. Set aside.

5. When cauliflower is tender, add the orecchiette pasta to the pot. Cook until al dente. Reserve a cup of pasta water.

6. Drain pasta and cauliflower and transfer to a large serving bowl. Cauliflower should have broken down more, and some of it should be almost like a cream. Add the bread and ½ cup of grated cheese. Toss to combine. Add a little olive oil to coat. Add some pasta water to moisten. Check seasoning and add salt if needed. Serve with extra cheese on the side.

VARIATION TIP: The ratio of these ingredients to each other can change and shift and still have a great result: less cauliflower, or more; less bread, or more; less cheese, or more. It's all good. You might also like to add a little hot pepper, which is a great addition if you like things spicy.

PAIR WITH: Spice-Rubbed Pork Tenderloin (page 106)

Farfalle with Grated Zucchini and Cream

SERVES: 4 to 5 | **PREP TIME:** 10 minutes | **COOK TIME:** 15 minutes

A friend of mine in New York who used to be a restaurant cook (and then a celebrated composer), gave me this recipe. Once I tried it, I cooked it every week—especially when zucchini was in season and in abundance. Calling for only a few ingredients, this is a meal that's at once delicate and light, deep and full-flavored.

Salt

1 pound farfalle (bow tie) pasta

2 tablespoons unsalted butter

2 tablespoons extra-virgin olive oil

1 medium onion, diced

2 medium zucchini, trimmed and grated

¼ cup dry white wine

½ cup heavy cream

Grated Parmesan, for serving

1. Heat 4 quarts of water in a pasta pot or large saucepan until boiling. Add 1 tablespoon of salt, and the pasta.

2. Heat the butter and oil in a large sauté pan with about 2-inch sides (to hold pasta later). Sauté onion until soft, over medium-high heat, about 3 minutes. Add grated zucchini. Cook until zucchini is rapidly simmering; add the wine, cook 3 to 4 minutes, then add the cream. Let simmer till cream reduces a bit. Season with salt.

3. When pasta is done, drain and add to zucchini sauce, reserving ½ cup of the pasta water. Heat and coat pasta with zucchini sauce; cook for another 2 minutes. Add a bit of pasta water or olive oil (or even a bit of cream or butter) if too dry. Transfer to a serving platter. Sprinkle with some grated Parmesan. Bring some grated Parmesan to the table for individual servings.

PAIR WITH: Arugula-Radicchio Salad with Pears and Gorgonzola (page 36)

Penne with Roasted Cherry Tomato Sauce

SERVES: 4 to 6 | **PREP TIME:** 15 minutes | **COOK TIME:** 30 minutes

Why stand at the stove, when you can make a great tomato sauce on a baking sheet in the oven? Here, delicate cherry tomatoes roasted with fresh herbs and garlic become a caramelized, deeply flavorful pasta sauce. Feel free to make this recipe vegan by omitting the grated Parmesan cheese at the end.

1 pint cherry or grape tomatoes

3 cloves garlic, peeled and smashed

¼ cup extra-virgin olive oil

3 tablespoons dry white wine

1 teaspoon sugar

1 tablespoon salt, plus more to taste

3 sprigs fresh Italian parsley

3 sprigs fresh thyme

1 pound penne pasta

½ cup grated Parmesan (optional)

1. Preheat the oven to 400°F.

2. Line a sheet pan with foil. Toss the tomatoes and garlic with the oil and wine, and spread out in a layer in the pan.

3. Sprinkle the mixture with sugar. Season with salt to taste. Scatter the parsley and thyme over the tomatoes. Roast in the oven for about 30 minutes until the tomatoes are tender and starting to brown.

4. Meanwhile, bring 4 quarts of water to a boil in a pasta pot or large saucepan. Add 1 tablespoon of salt. Drop in the penne and cook until al dente, about 8 minutes, or according to package directions.

5. Spoon half of the tomato sauce into a large, shallow serving bowl. Add a few tablespoons of pasta water. Drain the penne and add it to bowl; top with the rest of the sauce and gently stir to coat. Serve with some grated Parmesan to pass around the table.

VARIATION TIP: You can roast the tomatoes for about 10 minutes longer, until they're more blistered and slightly charred. This will give an almost smoky flavor to the sauce.

PAIR WITH: Chicken Piccata with Lemon and Capers (page 100)

Linguine with Fra Diavolo Shrimp Sauce

SERVES: 4 to 6 | **PREP TIME:** 10 minutes | **COOK TIME:** 15 minutes

When you see the term *fra diavolo* in Italian cooking, you know something spicy is coming. This recipe has been in my family since forever, and it's a top favorite. We've cooked it with shrimp, with clams, with blue-claw crabs, and even with lobster. But shrimp was the first and is the most frequent star. Almost all shrimp you buy in the store is frozen. Be sure to thaw the shrimp before using it in this recipe.

3 tablespoons extra-virgin olive oil

1 pound raw shrimp, peeled and deveined, tails removed

Salt

3 garlic cloves, peeled and minced

1 teaspoon dried oregano

Leaves from 4 or 5 sprigs fresh Italian parsley, minced

½ teaspoon red pepper flakes (or to taste)

¼ cup dry white wine

1 (28-ounce) can crushed tomatoes

1 pound linguine

1. Heat 3 tablespoons olive oil in a large saucepan until hot.

2. Season shrimp lightly with salt. Add shrimp to pan with oil. Cook, tossing, until shrimp are almost cooked through and pink. Remove shrimp from pan to a plate and reserve.

3. Add garlic, oregano, parsley, and pepper flakes. Cook for 1 to 2 minutes. Add the wine. Let the wine evaporate. Add the tomatoes. Stir to combine. Season with salt. Simmer gently for 10 minutes.

4. Meanwhile, bring 4 quarts of water to a boil in a pasta pot or large saucepan. When boiling, add 1 tablespoon of salt. Drop in the linguine. Stir, keeping strands from sticking together until water comes back to a boil. Cook the linguine to al dente, about 8 minutes, or according to package directions.

5. When you add the linguine to the water, add the shrimp back to the sauce, then simmer gently until pasta is cooked, about 8 minutes more.

6. Drain the linguine and put it in a serving bowl. Add the sauce and shrimp. Stir to combine. Serve.

VARIATION TIP: Some Italian cooks believe you shouldn't add grated cheese to a seafood pasta dish, as the cheese might make the dish too salty. A tasty alternative is to sprinkle toasted bread crumbs on top of your serving. Just heat a little olive oil in a small frying pan, add ½ cup bread crumbs, and stir over medium heat until the bread crumbs are lightly toasted.

PAIR WITH: Lightly Fried Calamari (page 121)

Baked Spaghetti with Ricotta and Sausage

SERVES: 4 to 6 | **PREP TIME:** 35 minutes | **COOK TIME:** 30 minutes

What could be better than a casserole dish filled with hot, saucy pasta and oozy melted cheese? Spaghetti is an unusual and fun choice for this baked pasta recipe, giving you lots of noodles to play with. This preparation may take a little time, but it's so worth it. It's also great the day after you make it—if it doesn't get scarfed down first.

4 tablespoons extra-virgin olive oil, divided

1 medium onion, diced

1 (28-ounce) can crushed tomatoes

Salt

4 or 5 Italian sausages

1 pound spaghetti

1 pound mozzarella, shredded with a box grater

½ cup grated Parmesan, divided

Freshly ground black pepper

1. Preheat the oven to 400°F.

2. Heat 2 tablespoons olive oil in a medium saucepan. Sauté the diced onion until softened, about 3 minutes. Add the tomatoes. Season with salt and pepper. Stir to combine. Simmer for 10 minutes. Reserve.

3. Remove the sausage meat from the casings. Heat a tablespoon of olive oil in a large sauté pan. Break up the sausage meat and add to the oil, using a spatula to break the meat into smaller pieces as it cooks. Sauté the meat until browned, 4 to 5 minutes. Coat the sausage with a little tomato sauce. Set aside.

4. Bring 4 quarts of water to a boil in a pasta pot or large saucepan. Add 1 tablespoon of salt, and spaghetti. Cook until al dente. Drain and transfer to a large mixing bowl. Coat the pasta with some tomato sauce. Add the mozzarella. Add the cooked sausage meat and stir to combine. Blend in half of the grated Parmesan.

5. Spread a thin layer of sauce on the bottom of a casserole pan (9-by-13-inch or similar). Fill with the pasta mixture, and smooth evenly. Spoon a little sauce on top. Sprinkle with the rest of the grated Parmesan.

6. Bake for about 30 minutes until the surface is golden and bubbling. Let stand about 5 to 10 minutes before cutting into squares or scooping with a spoon to serve.

VARIATION TIP: You can try this recipe with almost any cut of pasta; penne or ziti would be my pick.

PAIR WITH: Sicilian Orange and Fennel Salad (page 33)

Baked Stuffed Pasta Shells

SERVES: 4 to 6 | **PREP TIME:** 30 minutes | **COOK TIME:** 30 minutes

Here's a real Italian American classic. It's a family-pleaser, a crowd-pleaser, and a great potluck dish. You can double and triple the amount easily to accommodate any number of servings.

2 tablespoons extra-virgin olive oil

1 small onion, diced

1 (28-ounce) can crushed tomatoes

Salt

12 ounces large pasta shells

8 ounces mozzarella

1 pound ricotta cheese

¾ cup grated Parmesan, divided

Freshly ground black pepper

1. Preheat the oven to 400°F.

2. Heat 2 tablespoons oil in a medium saucepan. Add onion, and cook until softened, about 2 to 3 minutes. Add the tomatoes; season with salt and pepper. Simmer sauce for 10 minutes.

3. Meanwhile, bring 4 quarts of water to a boil in a pasta pot or large saucepan. Add 1 tablespoon of salt and the pasta shells. Cook the shells until al dente. Drain.

4. Grate the mozzarella using the large holes of a box grater. In a medium mixing bowl, mix together the ricotta, grated mozzarella, and ½ cup of the Parmesan. Season to taste with salt and pepper.

5. Put a few spoonfuls of tomato sauce in the bottom of a large casserole dish, enough to coat it completely. Holding one of the cooked pasta shells in your hand, fill it with the cheese mixture. Place it in the casserole dish with the opening facing up. Repeat with the rest of the shells, placing the filled shells in one layer. Spoon a light layer of tomato sauce over them. Sprinkle on the rest of the grated Parmesan.

6. Bake the shells in the oven until the cheese is golden and the shells are bubbling, about 30 minutes. Serve.

VARIATION TIP: These large shells just love to be filled. Try mixing in some cooked spinach with the cheese filling. Or make this a meat dish by filling the shells with cooked ground meat or sausage.

PAIR WITH: Broiled Lamb Chops with Salsa Verde (page 111)

Cast Iron Pan Pizza Margherita, page 78

6

Pizza, Breads,
and Focaccia

It seems there's always a basket or bowl of bread on the table at mealtimes in Italy. However, unlike Americans, Italians enjoy their bread plain or with food; there's no butter for slathering, nor oil for dipping. Bakeries, called *panetteria* (*pane* means "bread" in Italian), sell many shapes of bread and rolls, panini, focaccia, and pizza to go. Baked goods—sometimes sold by weight—are available throughout Italy, but you can make some of these Italian classic staples at home using the recipes in this chapter.

For fresh bread and pizza, there are the customary steps of making the dough, letting it rise, and then shaping and baking it. I've simplified the process as much as possible for the purpose of this book, and while these are not difficult recipes to follow, the rising process makes them time-consuming. Do not be put off by the length of some of these recipes; I wanted to include any detail that would be helpful for achieving a perfect end result.

In the following pages, you'll find a variety of pizzas: Grilled Pizza with Burrata and Fresh Tomatoes (page 76), Cast Iron Pan Pizza Margherita (page 78), and Sweet Pear Pizza with Brown Sugar and Sage (page 79). Make these recipes using store-bought dough, or try your hand at homemade pizza dough using the recipe on page 74. In this chapter, you'll also find an authentic focaccia recipe (page 83) from the region of Liguria. Other recipes are quick and inventive, such as Parmigiano Popovers (page 82) and Parmigiano Crackers (page 81). And there are even a few recipes that transform store-bought puff pastry into pizza and bread sticks, making it a snap to bring tasty breads to your Italian table.

Dad's Homemade Pizza Dough

MAKES: 4 10-inch pizzas, or 12 6-inch pizzas | **PREP TIME:** 20 minutes, plus 3 hours rising time

I watched my dad make this dough all through my childhood, and those memories are accompanied by the heady scent of yeast. The difference between this recipe and most other pizza doughs is one ingredient: egg—an addition somehow derived from my dad's Sicilian background. Making fresh dough is an adventure. The process is time-consuming, but the steps are easy to follow, and the results are incredibly rewarding.

5 cups all-purpose flour, plus extra for kneading

2 teaspoons salt

1½ cups warm water

2¼ teaspoons active dry yeast (one ¼-ounce envelope)

1 teaspoon sugar

¼ cup extra-virgin olive oil, plus 1 teaspoon to coat the dough

1 large egg

1. In a large mixing bowl, whisk together the flour and salt. In a medium bowl or large measuring cup combine 1½ cups warm water (tepid: not too hot, not too cool) with the yeast and the sugar; stir once gently. In a small bowl or cup, mix the olive oil with the egg.

2. Make a well in the center of the flour. When the yeast has "bloomed" (puffed up), pour the yeast water into the well. Pour the egg-and-olive-oil mixture into the well. With a large spoon, gently stir the flour and wet ingredients to roughly combine.

3. Start kneading the dough with your hands, pushing together the wet "rags" of dough until you have an amalgamated ball of dough. Then, take it out of the bowl and continue to knead on a clean work surface. If the dough is sticky, dust with extra flour (a quarter cup at a time) until you can handle it well. Knead for about 5 minutes until you have smooth ball of dough.

4. Smooth a thin film of olive oil all over the surface of the dough. Place the dough back in the bowl, or in another large mixing bowl. Cover top of bowl with 2 to 3 layers of clean dry kitchen towels. Leave the bowl of dough in a warm, draft-free place. Let rise about 2 hours. It will double in size.

5. After it rises, scoop the dough out onto a work surface. Using a knife or bench scraper, cut into four large pieces if you want to make approximately 10-inch pizzas. Or cut into 12 pieces for smaller, individual pizzas. Shape each piece into a ball by rolling it on your work surface. Wrap each ball loosely in an oil-sprayed or lightly oiled piece of plastic. Don't wrap it too tightly, since dough should continue to rise. Place wrapped balls on a sheet pan, and cover with a double layer of kitchen towels. Let rise about an hour more.

6. After dough balls rise a second time, they're ready to use in one of the recipes in this chapter. Or you can freeze them, wrapped in plastic. (Let the dough thaw and reach room temperature before shaping and baking.)

TIME-SAVING TIP: If you have a stand mixer, you can turn the kneading process into short work. Place the ingredients in the stand mixer bowl for steps 1 and 2. Using the dough hook, mix for about 3 to 4 minutes for step 3. Then, proceed with the rest of the recipe.

Grilled Pizza with Burrata and Fresh Tomatoes

SERVES: 4 to 6 | **PREP TIME:** 20 minutes | **COOK TIME:** 10 minutes

If you've got a grill, this is the easiest pizza you'll ever make. No grill? You can try this in your oven (see "Tip" below). But the fun part of this recipe is to let the crust get a little charred from the grill flames. How do you get a floppy piece of dough to cook on a grill? All it takes is a flick of the wrist. In this recipe I'm using *burrata* for a pizza topping, which is a cheese originating in the region of Puglia. It's similar to fresh mozzarella, except when you cut it open, a loose, creamy cheese spills out. If you can't find *burrata*, fresh mozzarella is a good substitute.

1 pound ready-made pizza dough (or ½ recipe Dad's Homemade Pizza Dough, page 74)

Extra-virgin olive oil, for drizzling

Nonstick cooking spray

3 cups cherry or grape tomatoes, halved

4 (2-ounce) balls burrata, quartered

Salt

1 cup baby arugula

1. Make sure your dough is at room temperature. It's easier to handle and stretch when it's not cold. Cut dough into 4 even pieces. Roll each piece into a ball. Gently press out into a circle. Stretch dough to make a bigger circle, 7 or 8 inches wide, by holding down the center and gently pulling the edges out. Lightly spread oil on the dough on both sides, and place on a sheet pan, cookie sheet, plate, or pizza peel.

2. Spray the grill grate with nonstick cooking spray before heating. Heat the grill to medium hot. When hot, lift one edge of the dough with both hands. The rest of the dough will hang. In one quick, deliberate movement, place dough flat onto the grill grate.

3. Let cook for 3 to 4 minutes, until the dough stiffens and grill marks appear on the underside. Flip dough over using tongs, and pull off onto a plate, peel, sheet pan, or cutting board, cooked-side up. The cooked side will be the top of your pie.

4. Top your pizza: Drizzle a little olive oil, scatter the tomatoes, and place *burrata* pieces. Season with salt and drizzle a little more oil on top.

5. Using tongs, slide dough back onto grill for the bottom side to cook and the toppings to cook and melt. Cook until grill lines appear on bottom, some char marks appear along the sides, and the toppings are bubbling, about 5 minutes. Using tongs, slide finished pizza off onto plate or cutting board. Top with a handful of arugula.

VARIATION TIP: If you don't have a grill, use the same process with a sheet pan in a 450°F oven. Press the dough into a flattened circle and place it on a lightly oiled sheet pan. Bake until the dough is golden, then remove it from the oven and add the toppings. Return to oven and bake until the toppings bubble and the crust is browned on the edges.

PAIR WITH: Chickpeas with Sage and Crunchy Fennel (page 97)

‖‖ ‖‖‖

SALT

What to buy

There are many different kinds of salt in the grocery store, and some home cooks (like me) get attached to particular types and brands. I use kosher salt, because I find it has the best quality and is the most versatile in the kitchen. Regular "table" salt has very fine, cube-shaped granules and is much saltier than kosher salt. In contrast, kosher salt's snowflake-shaped granules adhere to food better, and it has less sodium per teaspoon than table salt.

Look for finer-grain kosher salt (salts labeled "coarse" are only good for broader uses, like salting pasta water, not for seasoning). I prefer Diamond Crystal brand, as it is lower in sodium than the Morton's brand, which makes it easier to control the seasoning of your food.

For last-minute seasoning, or garnishes for fresh-baked bread or focaccia, finishing salts are worth the splurge. My favorites are Trapani sea salts, Himalayan pink salts, and French grey salts.

How to use it

Salt can make the difference between a mediocre dish and one that pops with flavor. You never want anything to taste salty, but you need to season your dish enough to bring out its inherent flavors. Always taste a dish before adding salt, then add a little at a time until it reaches peak flavor.

‖‖ ‖‖‖

Cast Iron Pan Pizza Margherita

SERVES: 4 to 6 | **PREP TIME:** 10 minutes | **COOK TIME:** 15 to 20 minutes

Pizza *Margherita* is the pizza of Naples. It has the colors of the Italian flag—red, green, and white—and was created in honor of Queen Margherita of Italy. Traditionally, it's a thin round of dough using Italian "00" flour, San Marzano tomatoes, and buffalo mozzarella. But here we take some liberties and fashion the Italian flag pizza in a cast iron pan with similar ingredients that are easy to find. The result: delicious.

1 large garlic clove,
peeled and halved

Salt

1 cup canned crushed
tomatoes

½ pound ready-made
pizza dough (or ¼ recipe
Dad's Homemade Pizza
Dough, page 74)

Extra-virgin olive
oil, for drizzling

½ cup sliced
mozzarella cheese

3 or 4 fresh basil leaves

1. Preheat the oven to 425°F.

2. Add the garlic and some salt to the tomatoes and let it sit for flavors to combine as you work with the dough.

3. Make sure the dough is at room temperature; it's easier to handle than when it's cold. Gently press the dough out into a circle the size of a 9-inch cast iron pan (or press into a thinner round of dough for a 12-inch cast iron pan). You can also stretch dough by holding the center and gently pulling the edges out.

4. Heat the cast iron pan in the oven on the bottom rack until very hot, about 5 minutes. Take out of the oven. Drizzle a little bit of olive oil in the pan. Place the dough circle carefully in the pan—the pan is *hot*. Try to push the dough up the sides along the edges (use a spoon if needed and watch your fingers). Drizzle a little olive oil on top. Put pizza back in the oven.

5. When the dough is starting to brown on the bottom and bubbling up on the top—about 5 minutes—take it out of the oven. Poke bubbles with a knife to let out steam and let the dough deflate some.

6. Spoon crushed tomatoes to cover the whole top lightly. Place mozzarella slices on top. Season with salt. Drizzle a little olive oil on top.

7. Place the pizza back in the oven until the bottom and edges are browned and the top is bubbling—5 to 8 minutes.

8. Remove pan, and transfer pizza with a pair of tongs to a plate or cutting board. Garnish with basil leaves. Cut into wedges. Serve hot.

TECHNIQUE TIP: Pay extra close attention when handling the cast iron pan. It's hot, and there's a lot of movement in and out of the oven. When the pan is out of the oven, place a pot holder on the handle to remind yourself it's hot.

PAIR WITH: Caesar Salad with Garlic-Anchovy Dressing (page 37)

Sweet Pear Pizza with Brown Sugar and Sage

SERVES: 4 to 6 | **PREP TIME:** 15 minutes | **COOK TIME:** 20 minutes

This recipe is a riff on a sweet Tuscan classic that features grapes on pizza. Sweet and pizza don't seem to go together, but actually it's a perfect match. The savory ingredients, olive oil and sage, balance the sweetness of the two sugars. It makes a dessert that's light and not overly cloying. To get the best crunch, let the dough get crispy-brown around the edges when baking.

1 pound ready-made pizza dough (or ½ recipe of Dad's Homemade Pizza Dough, page 74)

2 Bartlett pears, peeled, cored, and thinly sliced

½ cup granulated sugar (or to taste)

¼ cup packed light brown sugar

8 to 10 fresh sage leaves

Extra-virgin olive oil, for drizzling

1. Preheat the oven to 400°F.

2. Make sure dough is at room temperature. Press and stretch out dough into a thin, flat disc or oblong shape. Lay dough on a lightly oiled, parchment-paper-lined baking sheet.

3. Place the pear slices in a design on top of the dough, pressing them in lightly. Leave a narrow border of dough on the outside edge. Sprinkle evenly with sugars. Sprinkle most of the sage but leave some to sprinkle when pizza is done, as garnish. Drizzle olive oil on top.

4. Bake about 20 minutes until crusty and golden. Garnish with reserved sage leaves. Cut into wedges or squares to serve.

VARIATION TIP: Feel free to swap out the pears for thinly sliced fresh peaches or apples, nectarines, or grapes. And you might like to switch the herb, too. Rosemary works just as well as sage in this recipe.

PAIR WITH: Venetian Scroppino (page 17)

Puff Pastry Pizza

SERVES: 4 to 6 | **PREP TIME:** 15 minutes | **COOK TIME:** 25 minutes

Super delicate and crispy, this thin, quick-to-make pizza will be an immediate favorite. All you need is a box of puff pastry from the store. I recommend an all-butter puff pastry, if possible. Check the ingredients on the box to see if butter is included instead of oil.

Flour for dusting

1 sheet frozen puff pastry, thawed

3 medium tomatoes, thinly sliced

½ cup grated mozzarella

½ cup pitted, kalamata olives

½ red onion, peeled and thinly sliced

2 teaspoons dried oregano

2 or 3 tablespoons extra-virgin olive oil

Salt

Freshly ground black pepper

1. Preheat the oven to 400°F.

2. On a lightly floured surface, roll out pastry sheet to about ⅛ inch thick. Place on a parchment-paper-lined, rimmed baking sheet.

3. Place the tomato slices on top in one layer, leaving an inch free around the edges as a border. Sprinkle evenly with the cheese, olives, onion, and oregano. Drizzle lightly with olive oil. Season with salt and pepper.

4. Bake in the oven for about 25 minutes until the pastry is golden. Cut into squares. Serve warm or at room temperature.

TECHNIQUE TIP: When rolling out the dough, try not to let the center get too thin; keeping the dough thickness even throughout will prevent under- or overcooking the crust.

PAIR WITH: Crispy Artichoke Hearts with Aioli Dip (page 19)

Parmigiano Crackers

SERVES: 4 to 6 | **PREP TIME:** 20 minutes, plus 1 hour to chill | **COOK TIME:** 20 minutes

You don't usually see crackers in Italian cooking, but these buttery, cheesy crackers capture Italian flavors in a fun, crunchy way. They have streaks of sun-dried tomato, making them pretty, too. The rolled-out dough looks like an intricate abstract painting. A pile of these are a great accompaniment to an *aperitivo*. Serve them at a cocktail party, or as a snack while watching TV.

¼ cup unsalted butter
(4 tablespoons), at
room temperature

1¼ cups grated Parmesan

½ teaspoon salt

¼ teaspoon freshly
ground black pepper

Pinch hot pepper, or to taste

1 egg, lightly beaten

¾ cup all-purpose flour

1 tablespoon minced
sun-dried tomato

1 tablespoon minced
fresh rosemary leaves

1. Place the butter, Parmesan, salt, pepper, hot pepper, and egg in a large mixing bowl. With a large mixing spoon, mash together the ingredients until well blended. Add the flour, sun-dried tomato, and rosemary. Mix till combined.

2. Knead dough into a neat ball. Cover with plastic wrap and refrigerate for about an hour.

3. Preheat the oven to 350°F.

4. Roll dough out on a lightly floured surface to about ⅛ inch thick. Using a small round cookie or biscuit cutter (1-inch to 1½-inch), cut out small circles. Place circles on a parchment-paper-lined baking sheet.

5. Bake for 15 to 20 minutes until golden. Let cool for about 10 minutes before serving.

VARIATION TIP: Switch out the rosemary or sun-dried tomatoes for other favorites like dried or fresh minced oregano, minced olives, or minced chives. If you have a hand mixer, use it to combine dough before kneading.

PAIR WITH: Peach Bellini (page 15)

Parmigiano Popovers

SERVES: 4 to 6 | **PREP TIME:** 15 minutes | **COOK TIME:** 50 minutes

I've given these popovers an Italian flair with the addition of Parmesan cheese. They are light, airy, and irresistible—lovely hot from the oven or at room temperature. Using a popover pan is perfect, but a muffin pan with medium-size cups will work, too—your popovers just won't rise as high. The recipe is for 6 medium-size popovers, or 12 mini-popovers.

2 tablespoons unsalted butter, divided

¾ cup flour, plus more for dusting the pan

½ teaspoon salt

¼ cup grated Parmesan

2 large eggs

1 cup milk

1. Preheat the oven to 425°F.

2. Melt a tablespoon of butter. Lightly coat the pan cups with butter, then dust them with flour, shaking out excess flour.

3. In a large mixing bowl, whisk together flour, salt, and Parmesan. In a separate medium mixing bowl, whisk the eggs, then whisk in the milk until well combined. Melt the other tablespoon of butter, let cool a minute, then whisk into the egg mixture.

4. Slowly whisk the egg mixture into the flour mixture. Continue to whisk until combined. Don't worry about making it absolutely smooth.

5. Spoon batter into prepared popover cups (or muffin cups) until each is about two-thirds full. Place in oven and bake for 15 minutes. Then turn oven temperature down to 350 degrees. Bake for about 35 minutes more, or until deep golden brown.

6. Remove popovers from pan to a cooling rack or plate. Poke a paring knife into the top of each one to allow steam to escape. Serve immediately or let cool a bit. They should be slightly hollow when pulled open. These are great slathered with butter or drizzled with honey (or both).

TIME-SAVING TIP: Feel free to make these a day ahead. Popovers can be gently wrapped in foil and refrigerated overnight; just reheat them right before serving.

PAIR WITH: Italian Wedding Soup with Mini Meatballs (page 29)

Riviera Focaccia with Rosemary and Olives

SERVES: 4 to 6 | **PREP TIME:** 15 minutes, plus 2 hours inactive rising time | **COOK TIME:** 20 minutes

One summer I stayed in the Riviera at a beautiful villa high in the hills. The town was tiny, with just one little store selling fresh bread and focaccia in the morning. By the time we got our rectangle of focaccia home from our 5-minute walk to the store, the paper bag was stained through with olive oil. Olive oil and focaccia are very good friends, so don't be intimidated by how much is called for in this fabulous Riviera-style bread.

2 cups all-purpose flour

1 teaspoon salt

¼ teaspoon freshly ground black pepper

1 teaspoon active dry yeast

½ teaspoon sugar

1 cup warm water

2 tablespoons plus ¼ cup extra-virgin olive oil, divided

Leaves from 2 to 3 sprigs fresh rosemary

½ cup of pitted kalamata olives, or favorite pitted olives

¼ teaspoon finishing salt, or regular salt

1. Combine the flour, salt, and pepper in a large mixing bowl. Whisk to combine. Place the yeast and sugar in a small mixing bowl; add 1 cup warm water. Stir once. When yeast puffs up (blooms), add 2 tablespoons olive oil.

2. Make a well in the center of the flour mixture. Pour in the wet ingredients. Whisk together gently until flour is all absorbed and the mixture looks smooth, 1 to 2 minutes. It will be a very wet, almost batter-like dough. Cover dough in bowl with a clean kitchen towel. Place in a warm, draft-free spot and let dough rise until doubled, about 1½ hours.

3. Pour ¼ cup of olive oil in a quarter-sheet pan or rimmed jelly roll pan (approximately 9-by-13-inches). Pour out the dough into the pan without folding it, using a spatula to help. Poke your fingers into some of the oil, so the dough won't stick as you poke down the dough to fill pan. Push it into the corners and try to even out the thickness all around. Poking the dough gives it the characteristic pocked surface of focaccia. Cover the dough with a piece of parchment paper and then a kitchen towel. Let rise about 30 minutes more.

4. Preheat the oven to 425°F.

5. When the dough has risen a second time, discard parchment paper. Poke your fingers to make impressions again; scatter the rosemary and olives over the surface, and sprinkle finishing salt on top. Bake focaccia in the hot oven for about 20 minutes until golden. Allow to cool a few minutes before loosening from pan with a spatula. Cut into squares or strips.

TECHNIQUE TIP: I usually cut off ½ inch of the edges all around, before cutting into squares or strips. The edges are sometimes too crunchy, but some people love that part the best.

PAIR WITH: Americano (page 16)

Sesame-Cheese Bread Sticks

SERVES: 4 to 6 | **PREP TIME:** 15 minutes | **COOK TIME:** 15 minutes

You see bread sticks all over Italy and in Italian restaurants everywhere else. In Italy they call them *grissini*, and they come thick, thin, plain, or with seeds. These bread sticks are very light, with a great crunch. The sesame seeds, cheese, and hot pepper play well together, making a fun punch of flavor. Serve them with appetizers, at the table for lunch or dinner, or just as a snack.

1 sheet puff pastry, thawed

1 egg

1–2 teaspoons water

¾ cup sesame seeds

½ cup grated Parmesan

1 tablespoon cayenne

Salt

**Freshly ground
black pepper**

1. Preheat the oven to 425°F.

2. On a lightly floured work surface, roll out puff pastry to about 50 percent bigger than the original sheet. Keep to a rectangle shape. Beat the egg with a teaspoon or two of water and brush lightly on the surface of the dough. Sprinkle sesame seeds and Parmesan evenly over the surface. Sprinkle the cayenne (according to taste) evenly, and season with salt and pepper.

3. Using a knife or pizza cutter, cut dough in half across the width of the dough. Then cut each section lengthwise into ½-inch strips.

4. Line a sheet/baking pan with parchment paper. Lift each bread strip and twist it a couple of times, then line it up on the sheet pan. Repeat with the rest of the strips of flavored dough (you'll probably need 2 sheet pans). Bake for 10 to 15 minutes until golden. Cool before storing. Bread sticks keep at room temperature, wrapped in foil, for as long as a week.

PAIR WITH: Chopped Caprese Salad with Balsamic Vinegar (page 35)

Quick Bread Loaf with Ricotta and Ham

SERVES: 4 to 6 | **PREP TIME:** 15 minutes, plus 15 minutes to cool | **COOK TIME:** 1 hour

This is a fun, cakey loaf to pair with savory dishes. It can be whipped up easily and keeps for 3 to 4 days, wrapped in foil at room temperature. If you don't have a loaf pan, try using an 8-by-8-inch "brownie" pan. It will probably take less time baking—watch for its color turning golden. I love to slather toasted slices of this bread with butter for a decadent snack.

1 tablespoon unsalted butter, for greasing the pan

1 cup grated Parmesan

2 cups all-purpose flour, plus more for flouring the pan

2 teaspoons baking powder

2 teaspoons salt

3 large eggs

½ cup extra-virgin olive oil

¼ cup heavy cream

½ cup ricotta

⅓ cup diced ham or salami

1. Preheat the oven to 350°F. Lightly butter and flour a 9-by-5-inch loaf pan. Shake out any excess flour.

2. In a large mixing bowl, whisk together the Parmesan, flour, baking powder, and salt until well combined.

3. In a separate medium mixing bowl, whisk together the eggs, olive oil, cream, and ricotta until well combined. Stir in the ham (or salami).

4. Gently whisk the wet ingredients into the dry ingredients, mixing until the flour mixture is completely absorbed. The batter will look a little spongy.

5. Add the batter to the loaf pan and smooth the surface.

6. Bake for 60 to 70 minutes until golden. Cool 15 minutes. Take out of the pan. Cool completely. Slice and serve.

PAIR WITH: The Antipasto Platter (page 18)

Eggplant Parmigiana,
page 92

7

Vegetables and Legumes

Italy is right in the middle of the map that delineates the Mediterranean Diet—a way of eating that's praised for all of its heart-healthy benefits. In this diet, there is less reliance on meat, and more emphasis on fresh vegetables and fruit, legumes, and the use of olive oil. Plus, those following the Mediterranean diet are encouraged to eat with the seasons, enjoying produce grown close to home, soon after it's picked from the fields. When you go to a produce market in Italy, each vegetable and fruit has a sign that announces its price and also its origin. Everything comes from Italy, but Italian shoppers want a more precise knowledge of where their food comes from. So, if you're buying tomatoes in a Venice market, the sign might say "Sicilia," or the artichokes might say "Puglia." Some signs simply say *Nostro*, meaning "ours," which means the vegetables were grown right in that region.

Vegetables play a large role in Italian cooking. And there are so many vegetables that are particularly Italian; for example, fennel, artichokes, escarole, zucchini, and broccoli rabe (also known as rapini). Italians have embraced tomatoes, eggplant, and peppers, too, all of which are exceptionally rich in vitamins and minerals. Legumes like lentils and chickpeas are well-loved in Italy, and the two recipes in this chapter, Garlicky Lentils with Fried Croutons (page 96), and Chickpeas with Sage and Crunchy Fennel (page 97), are tasty examples of how a simple, yet protein-rich food can become so full of flavor. Consider going Italian-style and making vegetables and legumes a larger portion of your dinner plate.

Roman Sautéed Peas with Pancetta and Onion

SERVES: 4 to 6 | **PREP TIME:** 10 minutes | **COOK TIME:** 10 minutes

I call these "Roman" peas because I learned the recipe in Rome. I was a college student, focused on a totally absorbing course load. But in between classes, hallway conversations with classmates always centered on food. My Italian culture professor described this recipe to me during one of those breaks, and I've been making it ever since. It's deceptively simple, but I can eat a whole bowl of these peas for lunch all on their own.

2 tablespoons extra-virgin olive oil, plus more for drizzling

⅓ cup diced pancetta

1 medium onion, peeled, halved, thinly sliced

¼ cup wine

1 pound frozen peas

¼ cup water

Salt

Freshly ground black pepper

1. Heat olive oil in a medium sauté pan. Add the pancetta. Cook until lightly browned, 2 to 3 minutes.

2. Add the onion and cook until softened, 3 to 4 minutes. Add wine. Let it simmer for a minute or so until mostly evaporated.

3. Add peas and ¼ cup of water. Cook until peas are thawed, about 3 minutes. Season with salt and pepper. Drizzle with a little olive oil. Serve.

VARIATION TIP: Sometimes I add bite-size pieces of asparagus to this recipe. Let the asparagus cook with the onion before adding the peas.

PAIR WITH: Chicken Piccata with Lemon and Capers (page 100)

ORGANIC VS. NONORGANIC

At the turn of the 20th century, Italian farms were all pretty much organic. Then 20th-century industrialization brought larger farming practices and pesticides to farms worldwide, including Italy, and the smaller organic farms lost their foothold in the food system. Thankfully, in recent years, demand for organic farming has returned, and a lot of Italian farms are reaching back to their original organic practices.

Here in America, more and more organic vegetables fill supermarket produce sections, and prices for organic vegetables are becoming competitive with that of their nonorganic (i.e., conventional) counterparts, making it possible for just about anyone to eat more healthfully. However, since not all organic produce fits into my budget, I try to buy organic for the items that are known to contain the most pesticides in conventional produce, such as celery, carrots, and spinach.

Roasted Asparagus with Shallot and Parmigiano

SERVES: 4 to 6 | **PREP TIME:** 10 minutes | **COOK TIME:** 10 minutes

For all of the times I've cooked asparagus, it still feels like an "elegant" vegetable. I tried growing asparagus. When you see that single stalk pointing straight up from the ground, you have even more appreciation for what a wonder of a vegetable it is. I always cook asparagus simply. It has plenty of flavor on its own. You don't want to overcook it, though. Watch the color; it should still be bright green and crisp-tender when done.

1 bunch asparagus (about 1 pound) rinsed

Extra-virgin olive oil, for drizzling

1 shallot, peeled and diced

Salt

Freshly ground black pepper

¼ cup grated Parmesan

1. Preheat the oven to 400°F.

2. Cut off (or snap off) the woody ends of the asparagus and discard.

3. Line a medium baking pan with foil and drizzle a little olive oil to coat. Lay out the asparagus in one layer. Scatter the diced shallot over it. Season with salt and pepper. Drizzle olive oil lightly over asparagus.

4. Roast asparagus for about 10 minutes, until softened but still crisp-tender. Transfer asparagus to a serving platter. Sprinkle Parmesan on top. Serve.

INGREDIENT TIP: To find where to cut off or break the woody end of an asparagus spear: hold the tip end of the spear in one hand and the base in the other hand. Bend it until it breaks. The asparagus will snap right at the spot where the woody end begins.

PAIR WITH: Cod Acqua Pazza (page 115)

Asparagus Wrapped in Prosciutto with Crispy Bread Crumbs

SERVES: 4 to 6 | **PREP TIME:** 10 minutes | **COOK TIME:** 10 minutes

Prosciutto is probably the most prized of Italian cured meats. It's buttery, with a sweet-salty taste. When buying prosciutto, ask the deli counter to slice it very thinly. They should put deli paper between each slice to keep the thin slices from sticking to each other. You can also sometimes find prosciutto prepackaged in the refrigerated sections of stores like Trader Joe's, or in some supermarkets. The top brands imported from Italy are prosciutto di Parma, and San Daniele. But there are many other quality brands, too, like Boar's Head (not from Italy). In this recipe, two flavors make the perfect union: the grassy crunch of asparagus with the earthy embrace of the prosciutto.

Extra-virgin olive oil, for drizzling

1 pound asparagus, woody ends snapped off

Salt

Freshly ground black pepper

⅓ cup bread crumbs or panko bread crumbs

Zest of 1 lemon

1 tablespoon minced fresh Italian parsley leaves

¼ pound thinly sliced prosciutto

1. Preheat the oven to 375°F.

2. Line a sheet pan with foil. Drizzle a little olive oil. Add the asparagus and gently coat with the oil. Season with salt and pepper. Lay the spears out in one layer. Roast in the oven for about 10 minutes until done, ideally crisp-tender.

3. Meanwhile add a little olive oil to a small skillet and stir in the bread crumbs. Cook and stir until toasted to a golden color, 2 to 3 minutes. Remove bread crumbs to a medium mixing bowl. Add lemon zest and parsley. Season lightly with salt and pepper and stir to combine well.

4. To serve: wrap each asparagus spear in a slice of prosciutto and lay them out on a platter. Sprinkle with flavored bread crumbs.

INGREDIENT TIP: It's easy to make lemon zest. Use a small grater, a Microplane, or the smallest holes on a box grater. You want just the yellow part, so try not to grate too deeply into the white pith of the lemon (the pith is bitter). Lemon zest can wake up a lot of dishes.

PAIR WITH: Chicken Piccata with Lemon and Capers (page 100)

Broccoli Rabe with Garlic and Hot Pepper

SERVES: 4 to 6 | **PREP TIME:** 8 minutes | **COOK TIME:** 10 minutes

The Italian love affair with bitter points directly to broccoli rabe—also known as rapini. But the bitterness of this vegetable is its best quality. It's bright, assertive, and, in my opinion, *exciting*. The trick of first letting it cook in a little water helps tame the bitterness a bit. The addition of garlic and hot pepper flakes reflects the most traditional version of this recipe.

1 bunch broccoli rabe

⅓ cup water

Salt

3 or 4 tablespoons extra-virgin olive oil

3 garlic cloves, thinly sliced

½ teaspoon crushed red pepper, or to taste

Freshly ground black pepper

1. Cut the thick bottom stems off the broccoli rabe and discard. Cut the leaves and flowerets into smaller pieces: halving large leaves, and separating out floweret stems with a leaf or two attached.

2. In a large skillet, heat ⅓ cup of water till hot. Salt the water. Add the cut-up broccoli rabe. Cook at a lively simmer, until the broccoli rabe has wilted and the water has mostly evaporated, 3 to 4 minutes.

3. Add the olive oil, garlic, and crushed red pepper. Season with salt and pepper. Toss broccoli rabe in oil till coated. Cook until simmering, and broccoli rabe is tender to the bite, 3 to 4 minutes more. Serve.

INGREDIENT TIP: Many supermarkets sell broccoli rabe, but if you have trouble finding it, try this recipe with escarole. You can skip the addition of water and simply sauté in the oil with garlic and hot pepper.

PAIR WITH: Easy Beef Braciole with Garlic and Parmigiano (page 107)

Eggplant Parmigiana

SERVES: 4 to 6 | **PREP TIME:** 10 minutes | **COOK TIME:** 45 minutes

Sicily, Naples, and Emilia-Romagna all call this dish their own. Sicily is eggplant country. Emilia-Romagna is Parmigiano-Reggiano country, and Naples is mozzarella country. Often you see Eggplant Parmigiana bubbling under what seems to be a very thick layer of mozzarella. But parmigiana means Parmesan cheese, so that cheese should shine, too. Here's a version that's a little bit of both: a delicate amount of mozzarella *and* a good sprinkling of grated Parmesan.

2 medium eggplants

¾ cup all-purpose flour

Salt

Freshly ground black pepper

3–4 tablespoons extra-virgin olive oil, for sautéing

2 cups tomato sauce (see 15-Minute Tomato Sauce, page 58, or use store-bought)

½ cup grated Parmesan

8 ounces mozzarella, shredded

1. Preheat the oven to 375°F.

2. Peel eggplants with a potato peeler to remove the thin purply skin. Cut eggplants into ¼-inch rounds.

3. Place the flour in a medium-large shallow bowl, and season well with salt and pepper. Heat 3 to 4 tablespoons of oil in a large frying pan. When hot, dredge eggplant slices in flour, shake off excess, and fry until golden on each side, 3 to 4 minutes. Repeat with the rest of the slices, adding more olive oil to the pan if needed. Drain slices on a paper-towel-lined plate.

4. Add a thin layer of tomato sauce to a 9-by-13-inch casserole dish (or similar). Place one layer of eggplant slices at bottom. Coat lightly with tomato sauce. Sprinkle on some grated Parmesan and shredded mozzarella. Add another layer of eggplant; coat with a little sauce; add more of the cheeses. Repeat until all the slices and cheeses are used.

5. Bake for about 30 minutes until the casserole is bubbling and the cheeses are melted. Let stand 10 to 15 minutes before cutting into squares and serving.

INGREDIENT TIP: There's no need to salt the eggplant slices before using them in this recipe, since eggplant varieties of today are not really bitter. Plus, salting results in a very flat slice—and I prefer more bite to the eggplant. When buying eggplant, look for smooth, unblemished skin and fruits that feel hefty for their size.

PAIR WITH: Rustic Sausage Meatballs (page 105)

Roasted Sweet Baby Peppers with Oregano

SERVES: 4 to 6 | **PREP TIME:** 10 minutes | **COOK TIME:** 25 minutes

Do you know those multicolored little bell peppers they sell in small bags in produce departments? I was always drawn to their beautiful colors but didn't want to go through the trouble of cutting and cleaning them. Finally, I came up with a recipe that turns these peppers into delicious morsels without any fussy prep at all. These peppers are great as a side dish with meat or can be a pretty addition to an appetizer platter.

1 pound baby bell peppers (usually in assorted colors)

3 tablespoons extra-virgin olive oil

1 teaspoon dried oregano

Salt

Freshly ground black pepper

Leaves from 2 or 3 sprigs fresh oregano, minced

1. Preheat the oven to 400°F.

2. Put peppers in a medium mixing bowl. Drizzle them with olive oil and toss to coat the peppers. Sprinkle them with dried oregano. Season with salt and pepper. Mix to combine.

3. Lay peppers out in a single layer on a foil-lined, lightly oiled sheet pan.

4. Roast for 20 to 25 minutes, until softened and beginning to brown.

5. Transfer peppers to a serving platter. Sprinkle with fresh oregano. Serve.

PAIR WITH: Broiled Lamb Chops with Salsa Verde (page 111)

Sautéed Swiss Chard with Radicchio and Leek

SERVES: 4 to 6 | **PREP TIME:** 15 minutes | **COOK TIME:** 8 minutes

If you're not familiar with the leafy vegetables in this recipe, here's an opportunity to explore. In Italy, Swiss chard is called *bietole* and shows up in savory tarts and sautés, and red, slightly bitter radicchio is usually cooked or grilled, but is often used as a salad green, too. This simple sauté combines chard's subtle sweetness and radicchio's bite with the earthy flavor of leek, creating the perfect side dish for just about any meal.

1 leek

1 bunch Swiss chard (about 10 stalks)

½ head radicchio (about ⅓ pound)

2 tablespoons extra-virgin olive oil, for sautéing

Salt and freshly ground black pepper

1. Cut off the green end of the leek; use only the white part. Cut off the root. Cut leek in half lengthwise, and rinse under cool water, thumbing through the layers to clean well. Pat dry. Cut lengthwise again to get 4 long quarters. Cut across quarters into thin, small slices.

2. Rinse the Swiss chard and pat it dry. Gently rip the leaves of the Swiss chard from the ribs. (Discard ribs.) Tear or cut leaves into bite-size pieces. Cut radicchio into thin slices.

3. Heat 2 tablespoons of olive oil in a large sauté pan. When hot, add the cut-up leek. Sauté until softened and beginning to turn golden, about 4 minutes. Add the Swiss chard and radicchio. Cook at a lively simmer for 2 to 3 minutes, until leafy vegetables have wilted. Season with salt and pepper to taste. Serve.

INGREDIENT TIP: Swiss chard usually has a white rib running through its large, floppy leaves. But sometimes you find rainbow chard, with ribs that are yellow, red, and orange. All or any of these are worth trying in this recipe.

PAIR WITH: Roasted Salmon with Olives, Capers, and Herbs (page 116)

Butter-Braised Spinach with Slivered Almonds

SERVES: 4 to 6　|　**PREP TIME:** 3 minutes　|　**COOK TIME:** 6 minutes

I always have a bag of spinach in my crisper. I add it to soups, to stir-fries, and to eggs. But all on its own it's perfect. Spinach *tastes* green. You're getting a great dose of nutrition with a tender, delicate, silky consistency. In this recipe, butter and garlic make Popeye's hero-vegetable a real treat.

2 tablespoons
unsalted butter

1 garlic clove, peeled

9 ounces spinach, rinsed

Salt

⅓ cup slivered almonds

1. Heat the butter and garlic in a large sauté pan until butter has melted and starts to sizzle. Add the spinach, a little at a time, until each addition wilts and makes room for more. Turn with tongs to mix. Season lightly with salt. Cook until all the leaves are just wilted.

2. Stir in the almonds. Transfer to a serving bowl. Serve hot or at room temperature.

VARIATION TIP: The almonds in this recipe add some crunch and another layer of flavor. But you can leave them out, if you don't have any on hand—or swap slivered almonds for sliced almonds or pine nuts.

PAIR WITH: Roasted Cod with Crispy Parmigiano Crumbs (page 114)

Garlicky Lentils with Fried Croutons

SERVES: 4 to 6 | **PREP TIME:** 10 minutes | **COOK TIME:** 25 minutes

I learned this recipe years ago from my Roman roommate, Enrica. It's homey, cozy, and layered with flavor. When using dried lentils, I first spread them out on a sheet pan to look them over. It doesn't happen often, but occasionally you'll find a small stone in the mix. Better to check first. Also, this recipe is for brown lentils. Sometimes you find red or orange lentils, which are lentils without the hull. They cook faster, but also break down into a pea-soup consistency. Brown lentils work best for this recipe.

4–6 tablespoons extra-virgin olive oil, for drizzling and sautéing, divided

1 small onion, peeled and diced

3 garlic cloves, peeled, divided

1 cup dried brown lentils, picked over for any small stones, and rinsed

3 cups water

Salt

Freshly ground black pepper

3 to 4 slices Italian bread

1. Heat 2 to 3 tablespoons olive oil in a medium saucepan. Add the onion and 1 garlic clove. Cook until onion is softened, 3 to 4 minutes. Add the lentils. Cook until lentils are coated with oil and hot. Add 3 cups water. Season with salt and pepper. Bring to a simmer. Partially cover, and simmer until lentils are tender, about 20 minutes. If the water is absorbed before lentils are tender, add a little more water to the cooking.

2. Meanwhile, cut the Italian bread slices into bite-size squares or triangles. Heat 2 to 3 tablespoons olive oil in a medium frying pan. Add remaining 2 garlic cloves. When oil is hot, fry the bread with the garlic until slices are golden. Remove to paper-towel-lined plate. Discard garlic.

3. To serve, spoon some lentils into an individual serving bowl. Top with a few pieces of fried bread. Drizzle with a little olive oil.

TIME-SAVING TIP: If you can find canned lentils, you'll shave off some cooking time by using them instead of the dried lentils in this recipe. Just sauté the onion and garlic, then heat the cooked lentils on top and proceed with the remaining steps.

PAIR WITH: Italian Mixed Green Salad with Parmigiano Vinaigrette (page 32)

Chickpeas with Sage and Crunchy Fennel

SERVES: 4 to 6 | **PREP TIME:** 15 minutes

Chickpeas are a great vegetarian protein source that can add a "meaty" presence, texture, and body to almost any dish. You can buy chickpeas dried, then soak and cook them until tender. However, the canned version is just as good, a snap to access, and sold everywhere. This dish makes chickpeas the star of the show, contrasting their tenderness with some crunchy fennel and simple seasonings.

1 (15-ounce) can chickpeas

½ bulb of fresh fennel

1 shallot, peeled and diced

¼ cup fresh sage leaves, minced

Extra-virgin olive oil, for drizzling

Salt

Freshly ground black pepper

1. Drain the can of chickpeas into a colander and rinse them. Drain well. Add the chickpeas to a medium mixing bowl.

2. Cut off the top green stems of the fennel. Cut a slice from the bottom of the core (which is usually browned from its first cutting). Pull off and discard the outer thick layer. Cut remaining heart of fennel into quarters. Then cut across each quarter into thin slices.

3. Add the fennel slices, shallot, and sage leaves to the chickpeas. Drizzle olive oil over the top. Season with salt and pepper to taste. Stir well to coat. Serve.

INGREDIENT TIP: Fennel is sometimes called anise, though they are actually two different plants. If you can't find it, celery is a good substitute.

PAIR WITH: Red and Green Pepper Frittata (page 42)

Roman Lamb Abbacchio with
Roasted Potatoes, page 110

8

Poultry and Meats

Meat is treated as a precious element in Italian cooking. It doesn't take over the central place on the plate; instead, it's valued for its quality, not quantity. Lamb, veal, and pork are the most favored types of meat in Italy. Lamb is most popular in Rome, especially in the classic dish, Roman Lamb Abbacchio with Roasted Potatoes (page 110). Veal is popular in most Italian regions, but since it can be quite expensive, you'll only find one use for it in this chapter: the beloved classic, Veal Osso Buco Braised in Red Wine (page 108). Perhaps the most prevalent meat used in Italian cooking is pork, which makes up a large percentage of *salumi* (cured meats) like salami, *sopresatta*, and coppa. Fresh Italian sausage originated in the region of Basilicata, but is made in many variations throughout Italy—usually by mixing ground pork with pork fat, spices, and seasonings and stuffing the mixture into casings. In this chapter, I've included two of my favorite uses for fresh sausage: One-Pan Sausage and Peppers (page 104) and Rustic Sausage Meatballs (page 105).

Of course, Italians also cook with leaner meats, such as chicken and pork tenderloin, and you will find a delicious selection of applications for them in this chapter, too. Just remember: in Italian meals, meat is more like a side than the main event, meant to complement the other components on the plate rather than draw the spotlight.

Chicken Piccata with Lemon and Capers

SERVES: 4 to 6 | **PREP TIME:** 15 minutes | **COOK TIME:** 20 minutes

You often find this classic dish in Italian restaurants, but sometimes served with veal instead of chicken. Since chicken is easier to find, and easier on the budget, I prefer chicken—the savory flavors of lemon, butter, and capers shine through beautifully.

3 boneless, skinless chicken breasts

1 cup all-purpose flour

Salt

Freshly ground black pepper

2 tablespoons extra-virgin olive oil

2 or 3 tablespoons unsalted butter, divided

1 shallot, peeled and minced

Juice of 3 lemons

½ cup white wine

1 lemon, thinly sliced

2 tablespoons capers

1. Cut each chicken breast across its width into 5 or 6 quarter-inch-thick slices. Lay out six slices at a time, in one layer, on a sheet of plastic wrap. Cover with another piece of wrap. Lightly pound each slice with a meat pounder until slightly thinner and larger. Repeat with the rest of the slices.

2. Place the flour in a medium shallow bowl and season it with salt and pepper to taste. Heat the oil and 1 tablespoon butter in a large sauté pan. Dredge chicken slices/cutlets in the seasoned flour and shake off excess. Sauté the cutlets until golden on each side and cooked through. Add a little more oil if needed as you sauté. Lay out cooked chicken slices on a serving platter and tent with foil to keep warm.

3. Add the shallot to the same pan and cook till softened, about 1 minute. Add the lemon juice, wine, lemon slices, and capers. Cook for 2 to 3 minutes. Swirl in 1 or 2 tablespoons butter. Season with salt. Bring to a simmer. Pour over chicken. Serve.

TIME-SAVING TIP: To save time and work, you can often find chicken breasts already cut into cutlets at your supermarket. Also, take care working with raw chicken; it's known to transmit salmonella when raw. Wash hands and tools well after handling.

PAIR WITH: Baked Rice with Peas and Celery (page 49)

|||| |||||||/|||| |||||||/|||| |||||||/||||||||||||/|||||||||||||||||||||||/||| |||||||/||| |||||||/||| |||||

TIPS FOR COOKING MEAT

Tougher cuts of meat—generally parts of the animal that are high-activity muscles—are best cooked with moist heat, like braising. Braised meat cooks slowly at a simmer in broth, wine, or water, usually for about 2 hours to become tender. Veal Osso Buco Braised in Red Wine (page 108) is a great example, as is Easy Beef Braciole with Garlic and Parmigiano (page 107).

More tender cuts of meat are cooked quickly with dry heat—not in a liquid. They are pan-fried, grilled, or broiled, as in Broiled Lamb Chops with Salsa Verde (page 111). Chicken breasts are tender and cook more quickly than the dark meat of the higher-activity muscles in the legs and thighs.

Searing meat before braising or roasting it is a great way to get more flavor. The seared edges caramelize, creating an almost sugar-browned crust. Let meat rest for about 10 minutes after roasting, broiling, or grilling, so that the juices have time to settle back into the meat.

|||| |||||||/|||| |||||||/|||| |||||||/||||||||||||/|||||||||||||||||||||||/||| |||||||/||| |||||||/||| |||||

Chicken Saltimbocca with Sage and Prosciutto

SERVES: 4 to 6 | **PREP TIME:** 15 minutes | **COOK TIME:** 15 minutes

You can buy chicken cutlets, already sliced, in the supermarket. But I usually take a boneless, skinless chicken breast, slice it crosswise into about 5 slices, then lightly pound each slice. For this recipe, 2 or 3 chicken breasts make about 12 slices.

10 to 12 thin slices of chicken cutlet

Salt

10 to 12 thin slices of prosciutto

10 to 12 large sage leaves

10 to 12 toothpicks

½ cup all-purpose flour

Freshly ground black pepper

3–4 tablespoons extra-virgin olive oil, for sautéing

1. Place the slices of chicken on a platter. Season the cutlets with salt. Place a slice of prosciutto over each piece and one sage leaf on top. Weave a toothpick through the meat, prosciutto, and sage leaf to hold them together.

2. Place the flour in a medium bowl and season with salt and pepper to taste.

3. Heat olive oil in a large skillet. Dredge the meat in the seasoned flour and shake off excess. When oil is hot, add the chicken pieces, sage leaves down. Let cook 3 to 4 minutes until the prosciutto has a golden color. Turn the cutlets and cook 2 to 3 minutes on the other side until cooked through. Repeat with all cutlets, adding a little more olive oil to pan if needed.

4. Transfer to a platter. Serve.

INGREDIENT TIP: Take care working with raw chicken, it's known to transmit salmonella when raw. Wash hands and tools well after handling.

PAIR WITH: Soft and Cheesy Polenta with Roasted Mushrooms (page 40)

Pan-Roasted Chicken with Onion Pilaf

SERVES: 4 to 6 | **PREP TIME:** 15 minutes | **COOK TIME:** 50 minutes

A one-pan meal is always inviting. Here, the juices of the chicken flavor the rice and onions, and all you have to do is place them together. Bouillon cubes are usually a no-no in any chef's cooking, but in Italy I've seen many home cooks use a pinch here and there to boost the flavor of chicken. If you want to try this little trick, crumble a half bouillon square into the water you add to the pan.

Extra-virgin olive oil, for drizzling

½ cup rice (short or long grain)

1 medium onion, peeled and sliced

Salt

Freshly ground black pepper

1 whole chicken (3 or 4 pounds)

1 cup water

Pinch powdered bouillon (optional)

2 or 3 sprigs fresh rosemary

1. Preheat the oven to 400°F.

2. Use a 9-inch or 12-inch cast iron pan. Pour a thin film of olive oil over the bottom. Pour in the rice, scatter the onion, and season with salt and pepper.

3. Drizzle the chicken with a little olive oil. Season well with salt. Place chicken on top of rice mixture. Add 1 cup water. Add a pinch of bouillon cube, if using. Drizzle a little olive oil over the rice. Add the rosemary sprigs.

4. Place the pan in the oven. Cook for about 50 minutes, until an instant-read thermometer reads 165 or higher when stuck into the thigh meat. During cooking, if water evaporates, add a little more. When done, cut chicken into pieces. Serve with rice and onions.

PAIR WITH: Sicilian Orange and Fennel Salad (page 33)

One-Pan Sausage and Peppers

SERVES: 4 to 6 | **PREP TIME:** 15 minutes | **COOK TIME:** 40 minutes

This dish reminds me of the San Gennaro Festival in New York's Little Italy that takes place every fall. The streets are decorated with green, white, and red lights, closed to traffic, and lined with food stands selling everything from pizza to zeppole to calzones. But the food filling the air with the most irresistible aroma is sausage and peppers. The mixture sizzles on the griddle, ready to be stuffed into a roll or eaten straight with a fork. This recipe re-creates that festival taste right in your kitchen.

2 medium onions

3 red or green bell peppers, or a mixture

6 to 8 Italian sausages

Extra-virgin olive oil, for drizzling

Salt

Freshly ground black pepper

1. Preheat the oven to 400°F.

2. Peel the onions and cut them into ½-inch wedges. Cut the peppers in half. Pull out the stem and seeds. Cut the peppers into ½-inch strips.

3. Using kitchen scissors, cut each sausage into 3 or 4 pieces (you can use a knife, but scissors are easier with raw sausages).

4. Line a sheet pan with foil. Drizzle some olive oil to lightly coat. Sprinkle cut onions and peppers over the pan. Scatter the sausage pieces. Drizzle a little olive oil over everything. Season with salt and pepper to taste.

5. Roast in the oven for about 40 minutes until vegetables and sausage are cooked through and starting to brown. Turn vegetables and sausages 1 to 2 times while cooking.

6. Serve hot or warm on a large platter.

PAIR WITH: Spaghetti with Spicy Aglio e Olio (page 60)

Rustic Sausage Meatballs

SERVES: 4 to 6 | **PREP TIME:** 15 minutes | **COOK TIME:** 20 minutes

When you buy Italian sausages in the store, sometimes you have the choice of sweet or hot. Sweet just means they're not spicy (don't worry—there's no sugar involved). Hot Italian sausages bring just the right amount of heat. For this recipe you can choose either, depending on your preference. Since Italian sausages are already seasoned with some spices, they're flavorful right from the start.

1½ pounds Italian sausage meat, or 5 or 6 Italian sausages, casings removed

¼ cup fresh Italian parsley leaves, minced

Salt

Freshly ground black pepper

1. Preheat the oven to 375°F.

2. Place the sausage meat and parsley in a medium mixing bowl. Season lightly with salt and pepper. With a large spoon, or your hands, mix until well combined.

3. Line a sheet pan with foil. Make 1-inch or 2-inch balls of meat mixture and line them up on the sheet pan.

4. Roast for about 20 minutes until cooked through and golden.

VARIATION TIP: Meatballs are the perfect canvas for adding extra flavors. In Naples they add pine nuts and raisins. Or, you could add a little minced garlic, other fresh herbs, or minced, sun-dried tomatoes.

PAIR WITH: Penne with Roasted Cherry Tomato Sauce (page 67)

Spice-Rubbed Pork Tenderloin

SERVES: 4 to 6 | **PREP TIME:** 8 minutes | **COOK TIME:** 35 minutes

Pork tenderloin is such an easy cut to cook, and makes relatively fat-free tender slices of meat. Because tenderloin is much thinner than a larger pork loin, it only takes about a half hour to roast. This simple dry rub ups the flavor and succulence. I chose some of my favorite spices here, but feel free to mix it up and substitute your favorite flavors.

2 teaspoons sweet paprika

2 teaspoons crushed red pepper or 1 teaspoon cayenne

2 teaspoons ground cumin

1 teaspoon ground fennel or fennel pollen

Salt

2 pork tenderloins, about 1 pound each

2–3 tablespoons extra-virgin olive oil, and more for drizzling

2 medium onions, peeled and quartered

1. Preheat the oven 375°F.

2. In a small mixing bowl mix together the paprika, crushed red pepper, cumin, fennel, and a few healthy shakes of salt. Rub the spice mix all over the meat.

3. Heat tablespoons olive oil in an ovenproof casserole or skillet with at least 2-inch sides. Sear and brown the pork on all sides, about 5 minutes.

4. Scatter onions around the pork. Transfer the casserole uncovered to the oven. Roast for about 30 minutes, until an instant-read thermometer reads 145.

5. Take pork out, tent with some foil, and let rest for about 10 minutes before cutting. There will be some "carry-over" cooking as the meat rests. Cut into thin slices, serve with the onions and juices.

TECHNIQUE TIP: When you slice across the pork, you make small, round slices. Slice across on a diagonal for longer, oval-shaped slices.

PAIR WITH: Roasted Sweet Baby Peppers with Oregano (page 93)

Easy Beef Braciole with Garlic and Parmigiano

SERVES: 4 to 6 | **PREP TIME:** 20 minutes | **COOK TIME:** 1 hour

During my first trip to the region of Puglia, I had the happy occasion to cook with a grandmother in her home. We made fresh pasta and this very easy *braciole*. My family makes *braciole*, too, but this Pugliese version was so different and much simpler (every region and every family has their own version). Basically, thin pieces of beef are stuffed and rolled, then braised in tomato sauce. Another surprise: she put the just-rolled *braciole* into a pan with cold oil, then put it on the heat to cook. I had never seen that before. Usually, you heat the oil before adding meat. But this worked beautifully, which was a revelation.

6 thin pieces of beef, like thin-sliced sirloin tip, each about 4 inches by 4 inches

6 (1-inch) chunks Parmesan cheese

3 large garlic cloves, peeled and cut in half

12 flat-leaf Italian parsley leaves

6 toothpicks

3–4 tablespoons extra-virgin olive oil

¼ cup dry white wine

1 (28-ounce) can crushed tomatoes

Salt

1. Lay the pieces of beef out flat on a clean work surface. Place a piece of cheese, a piece of garlic, and 2 parsley leaves in the center of the bottom third of each slice. Roll up the beef around the cheese-garlic-parsley, so you have a "jelly roll" of beef. Secure the end by threading a toothpick to keep it closed. Repeat with all the beef slices.

2. Pour the oil in a large saucepan that can hold the rolled beef in one layer. Place the meat in the pan, and then put it on the stove to heat. Start at medium until the meat starts to simmer. Cook at a lively simmer until meat is browned on all sides, about 5 minutes.

3. Add the wine. Let some evaporate, then add the tomatoes. Season with salt to taste. Cook, with cover askew, at a slow simmer, for about 1 hour or longer, until the meat is easy to cut. Serve.

VARIATION TIP: You can make this dish into a full meal by adding pasta. Boil your favorite pasta and use with the braising tomato sauce. Serve with the meat.

PAIR WITH: Sautéed Swiss Chard with Radicchio and Leek (page 94)

Veal Osso Buco Braised in Red Wine

SERVES: 4 to 6 | **PREP TIME:** 20 minutes | **COOK TIME:** 2 hours and 15 minutes

Osso buco is a classic dish from the Lombardia region of Italy. They are slices of veal shank (the lower leg). *Osso* means bone in Italian, and *buco* means hole. The shank slice is a circle with a round bone in the middle. There's a hole in the bone filled with marrow. It's a prized delicacy to eat the marrow with a little spoon. You will probably have to order the cut from a butcher. It does take some braising time, but it's not difficult to make—an impressive dish to serve guests. The addition of the traditional *gremolata* gives the meat a bright accent.

FOR THE OSSO BUCO

6 veal shank slices

3–4 tablespoons extra-virgin olive oil

½ cup all-purpose flour

Salt

Freshly ground black pepper

2 carrots, diced

2 celery stalks, diced

1 onion, peeled and diced

2 cups red wine

1–2 cups low-sodium beef or chicken broth

TO MAKE THE OSSO BUCO

1. Tie kitchen string around the outside of the meat of each slice of veal. This helps keep the meat on the bone as it cooks.

2. Heat the olive oil in a heavy casserole pot or heavy-bottomed pan with at least 2-inch sides. Place the flour in a medium bowl and season it with salt and pepper. When the oil is hot, quickly dredge the shanks in the seasoned flour, shaking off excess. Brown the shanks on all sides, about 8 minutes. Take the meat out of the pan.

3. Add the carrots, celery, and onion. Add more oil if needed. Sauté until softened, 4 to 5 minutes. Add the wine. As it sizzles, scrape up any browned bits from the bottom of the pan. Add 1 cup of broth. Return the meat to the pan and bring up to a simmer. Season with salt.

4. With pan cover askew, let braise at a simmer for about 2 hours. Gently turn the meat halfway through cooking. Add more broth if too much liquid is evaporating. When done, meat should be fork-tender.

2 teaspoons lemon zest

2 tablespoons Italian parsley, minced

3 garlic cloves, peeled and minced

Extra-virgin olive oil, for drizzling

Salt

TO MAKE THE GREMOLATA

Meanwhile, make the gremolata: in a small mixing bowl, mix together the lemon zest, parsley, and minced garlic. Add a little olive oil and a little salt.

TO FINISH THE DISH

When the meat is done, let meat rest in the sauce for about ten minutes before serving. Transfer each shank to a serving dish and remove the string. Spoon a little cooking juice on top of each piece. Then, top with a small spoonful of gremolata.

PAIR WITH: Risotto Milanese with Saffron (page 48)

Roman Lamb Abbacchio with Roasted Potatoes

SERVES: 4 to 6 | **PREP TIME:** 15 minutes | **COOK TIME:** 30 minutes

Traditionally, this dish is made with baby (suckling) lamb, and it is the quintessential springtime dish in Rome. However, the recipe works just as well with the lamb you can find easily in supermarkets. Here, you cut shoulder lamb chops into smaller pieces. You end up with odd pieces of lamb and odd pieces of bone, but that is as it should be. The roasted potatoes absorb the meat juices, making this a perfect comfort food.

8 lamb shoulder chops (blade or with round bone)

Salt

Freshly ground black pepper

2–3 tablespoons extra-virgin olive oil, plus more for drizzling

1 medium onion, peeled and sliced in half circles

4 garlic cloves, peeled and chopped

5 or 6 red potatoes, peeled, cut into ¼-inch slices

⅓ cup mild vinegar

3 to 4 rosemary sprigs, plus 1–2 sprigs for garnish

1. Preheat the oven to 375°F.

2. Cut lamb chops into 2 to 3 pieces per chop. Season with salt and pepper.

3. Heat olive oil in a large roasting pan, Dutch oven, pot, or skillet that can go in the oven. Sear the lamb pieces until well browned. Remove. Add the onion, garlic, and potatoes. Cook for 3 to 4 minutes until vegetables have softened a little. Add back the lamb. Drizzle the chops with vinegar and some olive oil. Add 3 or 4 rosemary sprigs. Season some more with salt and pepper.

4. Roast in oven for 20 to 25 minutes for medium-well doneness (and until potatoes are tender). Roasting time can vary, depending on your preference for rare or well-done meat. Traditionally, lamb is served cooked rare to medium-well.

5. Transfer lamb, potatoes, and onions to a serving platter. Garnish with reserved rosemary sprigs. Serve hot.

PAIR WITH: Roman Sautéed Peas with Pancetta and Onion (page 88)

Broiled Lamb Chops with Salsa Verde

SERVES: 4 to 6 | **PREP TIME:** 15 minutes, plus 1 hour marinating time | **COOK TIME:** 10 minutes

Lamb chops are quick-cooking and super-savory. If you want to save time, skip the marinating part of this recipe. Season the chops well with salt and pepper and get them right into the oven. 15 minutes later: dinner is ready. If you *do* have the time, the marinade will add an additional level of flavor. Salsa verde is one of those easy-to-make condiments that can take the dish to a "gourmet" level.

FOR THE LAMB

1 rack of lamb
(10 to 12 bones)

1 or 2 sprigs fresh rosemary

2 or 3 cloves of garlic,
peeled and smashed

¼ cup extra-virgin olive oil

Salt

FOR THE SALSA VERDE

1 cup Italian parsley
leaves, minced

¼ cup capers

2 or 3 tablespoons
extra-virgin olive oil

Pinch hot pepper flakes,
or cayenne pepper

Salt

Freshly ground
black pepper

TO MAKE THE LAMB

1. Cut the lamb into individual chops. Trim off some of the fat, if you prefer. Add the chops, rosemary, garlic, and olive oil to a large ziplock bag. Press and move ingredients around to distribute. Let marinate in refrigerator for at least an hour and up to 3 hours.

2. Heat the broiler to medium-high with rack about 3 inches from the heating element. Remove lamb chops from marinade (discard marinade in bag). Lay chops out on a sheet pan. Season with salt on both sides. Place the pan under the broiler and cook chops 3 to 4 minutes per side.

TO MAKE THE SALSA VERDE

Meanwhile, make the salsa verde. In a medium mixing bowl, stir together the parsley, capers, and olive oil. Stir in hot pepper flakes. Season with salt and pepper to taste.

TO FINISH THE DISH

Serve lamb hot or warm. Use salsa verde as a condiment.

TECHNIQUE TIP: Instead of broiling, you can also grill these chops. Grill until golden and slightly charred on one side; turn and cook until golden and slightly charred on the other side—3 to 4 minutes per side.

PAIR WITH: Roman Sautéed Peas with Pancetta and Onion (page 88)

Roasted Salmon with Olives, Capers, and Herbs,
page 116

9

Fish and Seafood

Italy is a peninsula in the Mediterranean, Tyrrhenian, and Adriatic Seas with approximately 5,000 miles of coastline snaking along almost every region in the country. So, it's no surprise that fishing has always been a major industry in Italy, and that a vast majority of Italian homes enjoy the local catch—especially anchovies, sardines, mullet, shrimp, tuna, swordfish, and octopus. Italians are also fond of *baccala*, which is codfish preserved in Norway. Somehow this salt-preserved fish made its way to Italy, where it worked its way into the cuisines of Naples, Rome, and Venice. In this chapter, you'll find two recipes that give a nod to *baccala*, but instead use fresh codfish, which in Italy is called *merluzzo*. (See Cod Acqua Pazza, page 115, and Roasted Cod with Crispy Parmigiano Crumbs, page 114.)

Shrimp are also popular in Italy, where the most common species are called *gambero* or scampi, and of course no Italian cookbook would be complete without a recipe for Shrimp Scampi (page 119). Two other popular seafood options in Italy are the white-fleshed fish *orata* and *branzino* (sea bream and sea bass), but they are not easy to find outside of the country, so instead I used tilapia for their classic applications: poached in savory sauce (page 117) and baked in parchment packets (page 118). Mussels (*cozze*), crab (*granchio*), and squid (*calamari*) are all Italian favorites, too—you'll find my favorite savory and succulent recipes for each of them in this chapter.

Roasted Cod with Crispy Parmigiano Crumbs

SERVES: 4 to 6 | **PREP TIME:** 8 minutes | **COOK TIME:** 20 minutes

Traditionally cheese and fish don't go together in Italian cooking. However, I've learned that's mostly true in the region of Campania. Fish dishes in Venice often have added cheese. When this cod comes out of the oven, the combination of grated Parmesan with crispy panko crumbs tastes deep and buttery, when no butter has been added—just olive oil.

4–5 tablespoons extra-virgin olive oil

6 cod fillets (about 4 ounces each)

Salt

Freshly ground black pepper

½ cup grated Parmesan

½ cup panko or bread crumbs

1. Preheat the oven to 400°F.

2. Lightly oil a foil-lined sheet pan. Season the fish with salt and pepper and place on pan.

3. In a small mixing bowl mix together the Parmesan and bread crumbs. Season with a little salt and pepper, and moisten with a little olive oil until you have a wet-sand consistency. Pile crumbs on top of each fillet. Drizzle a little olive oil on top.

4. Bake in oven for 15 to 20 minutes until fish is cooked through and bread crumbs are golden.

PAIR WITH: Roasted Asparagus with Shallot and Parmigiano (page 89)

||||| |||||||||||| ||||||||||||||||||||||||||||||||||||||||||||||| ||||||||||||||| ||||||||||||| |||||||

TIPS FOR BUYING AND COOKING FISH

When buying fish and other seafood items, try to check the country of origin. The organization SeafoodWatch.org lists recommended species and origins. Mainly, their recommendations take into consideration fish farming practices, overfishing, and which countries export the best product.

The best thing to keep in mind when cooking fish is that it doesn't need a lot of time. Steaming or poaching fish, as in Steamed Mussels with Cannellini Beans and Bacon (page 122) and Cod Acqua Pazza (page 115), is a foolproof way of keeping fish moist and instilling lots of flavor. The calamari on page 121 fries for just a minute.

The rule for squid: cook it superfast or superlong. If you go beyond that first quick minute, you end up with too-chewy squid that can only become tender with long braising.

Roasting fish in a medium oven for about 20 minutes concentrates its flavor and tenderness, as in Roasted Salmon with Olives, Capers, and Herbs (page 116).

||||| |||||||||||| ||||||||||||||||||||||||||||||||||||||||||||||||||| ||||||||||||||||| |||||||||||| |||||||

Cod Acqua Pazza

SERVES: 4 to 6 | **PREP TIME:** 10 minutes | **COOK TIME:** 20 minutes

Ravello is perched high in the hills of the Amalfi Coast in Campania. My traveling group and I took a cooking class with Chef Vincenzo at an open-air kitchen there. The view looked out over their small trunk garden and then out to sea at an elevation of 1,200 feet. We cooked a full lunch menu, including this fish *acqua pazza* style. *Acqua pazza* means "crazy water." The poaching liquid is made "crazy" with fresh tomatoes, garlic, parsley, and olive oil. Simple. Crazy simple.

3 large ripe tomatoes, coarsely diced

2 or 3 garlic cloves, peeled and minced

Pinch hot pepper

¼ cup minced Italian parsley

¼ cup extra-virgin olive oil

2 cups water

Salt

Freshly ground black pepper

6 cod fillets (about 4 ounces each)

½ baguette, sliced

1. In a large sauté pan with a cover, place the tomatoes, garlic, hot pepper, parsley, olive oil, and water. Season with salt and pepper. Cover and bring to a simmer. Let simmer for 10 to 12 minutes.

2. Take the cover off and let liquid boil until reduced to at least half, 2 to 3 minutes. Season the fish with salt. Add the cod fillets to the tomato mixture. Partially cover with a lid, and lower heat to a simmer. Cook until fillets are cooked through, 8 to 10 minutes.

3. Meanwhile, toast the bread slices in a toaster or oven until golden.

4. For individual servings, place a toasted bread slice at the bottom of a shallow soup bowl. Serve a cod fillet on top, with a couple of spoonfuls of tomato and tomato juices.

VARIATION TIP: You can make almost any fish "crazy." Use tilapia instead. Or even swap in shellfish like mussels or clams—using the same method, let them simmer in the broth until the shells open.

PAIR WITH: Panzanella Salad with Cucumbers (page 34)

Roasted Salmon with Olives, Capers, and Herbs

SERVES: 4 to 6 | **PREP TIME:** 10 minutes | **COOK TIME:** 20 minutes

Of the many types of salmon, the most common varieties are Atlantic, sockeye, and coho. Any of these are fine for this recipe. Olives and capers are the perfect flavors to go with this fish. Choose black or green olives that are already pitted. And my favorite capers are called nonpareils—they are the tiniest ones.

Extra-virgin olive oil, for drizzling

2 pounds skinless salmon fillet

Salt

Freshly ground black pepper

1 shallot, minced

3 to 4 garlic cloves, peeled

½ cup black or green olives, pitted and sliced

¼ cup capers

2 lemons

¼ cup minced fresh Italian parsley leaves

1. Preheat the oven to 400°F.

2. Line a sheet pan with foil. Drizzle a thin film of olive oil over it. Place the fish on top. Season fish lightly with salt and pepper. Sprinkle it evenly with shallot, garlic, olives, and capers. Drizzle a little olive oil on top.

3. Cut one of the lemons in half. Squeeze the halves over the fish. Cut the other lemon into small wedges. Set lemon wedges aside.

4. Roast the fish until cooked through, about 20 minutes. Transfer the fillet to serving platter. Garnish with reserved lemon wedges and parsley.

PAIR WITH: Farfalle with Grated Zucchini and Cream (page 66)

Tilapia Poached in Tomato-Tarragon Sauce

SERVES: 4 to 6 | **PREP TIME:** 10 minutes | **COOK TIME:** 25 minutes

Tomato sauce has an irresistible umami flavor; it's why it permeates so much of Italian cooking. So why not cook fish in it? This tomato sauce is deepened with a lively hint of tarragon, a fresh herb with a light anise-licorice flavor. In Italian it's called *dragoncello.* I grow it every summer in my herb garden and keep finding new ways to include it in recipes. To make this dish a full meal, serve it over cooked white rice.

2–3 tablespoons extra-virgin olive oil

1 small onion, peeled and diced

1 garlic clove, peeled and crushed

¼ cup dry white wine

1 28-ounce can crushed tomatoes

Salt

Freshly ground black pepper

2 teaspoons fresh tarragon, minced or 1 teaspoon dried tarragon

4 to 6 tilapia fillets

1. Heat the olive oil in a medium-large sauté pan. Add the onion and garlic. Cook until the onion softens. Add the wine. Let it evaporate. Add the tomatoes and season the mixture with salt and pepper. Stir in the tarragon. Simmer for 15 minutes.

2. Slip the tilapia fillets into the sauce. Spoon sauce over the top of the fish. Partially cover the pan. Simmer on medium-low for about 10 minutes until fish turns an opaque white.

3. Serve with a generous spoonful of sauce for each serving.

PAIR WITH: Sautéed Swiss Chard with Radicchio and Leek (page 94)

Baked Parchment Packets with Tilapia, Thyme, and Lemon

SERVES: 4 to 6 | **PREP TIME:** 20 minutes | **COOK TIME:** 15 minutes

Cooking food in parchment packets is like creating a microclimate for the ingredients. They're cooking in their own little world with flavors concentrating and marrying with each other. In these packets, the clean taste of tilapia is enhanced with shallot, tomatoes, butter, lemon, and wine. You see dishes in Italy like this; there they're called *al cartoccio*—"cooked in paper."

6 (4-ounce) tilapia fillets

Salt

Freshly ground black pepper

1 shallot, minced

6 to 8 cherry tomatoes, quartered

Extra-virgin olive oil, for drizzling and brushing

6 (12-by-16-inch) pieces of parchment paper

½ cup dry white wine

1 lemon, thinly sliced

6 tablespoons unsalted butter

6 thyme sprigs

1. Preheat the oven to 400°F.

2. Season the tilapia with salt and pepper. In a small mixing bowl, mix together the shallot and the tomatoes. Add a drizzle of olive oil, and season with salt and pepper.

3. Fold each piece of parchment paper in half to get a crease. Then open each sheet. Brush half lightly with olive oil.

4. Place a tilapia fillet on the oiled half of each parchment. Divide the shallot-tomato mixture to top each of the six fillets. Sprinkle each with a couple of teaspoons of wine. Drizzle lightly with olive oil. Add a lemon slice, a tablespoon of butter, and a sprig of thyme.

5. Fold over the parchment paper so that the ends meet evenly. Starting at one corner, make a small fold to close. Repeat, making small folds all around the opened edges until you have formed an enclosed semicircle. Press folds tightly. Tuck under the last corner. Brush each top with a little olive oil and place the packages in a single layer on a rimmed baking sheet.

6. Bake for 15 to 20 minutes. Serve each package on a dinner plate and let diners open their packages at the table. Careful; some hot steam can escape.

TECHNIQUE TIP: If you don't have parchment paper, use pieces of aluminum foil instead.

PAIR WITH: Caesar Salad with Garlic-Anchovy Dressing (page 37)

Shrimp Scampi

SERVES: 4 to 6 | **PREP TIME:** 10 minutes | **COOK TIME:** 15 minutes

Butter. Garlic. Shrimp. These three ingredients that make this classic Italian American dish such an enduring favorite. Growing up, this recipe was always the centerpiece of my family's Christmas Eve Feast of the Seven Fishes dinner. My parents bought very large shrimp for that night, and we all swooned over the flavors. But don't wait for a holiday. Once you learn how simple it is to make, any night can be Shrimp Scampi night.

1 pound large or jumbo shrimp, shelled and deveined

Salt

Freshly ground black pepper

1 stick (8 tablespoons) unsalted butter

¼ teaspoon crushed red pepper flakes or cayenne pepper

3 garlic cloves, chopped

1 large shallot, chopped

3 to 4 tablespoons extra-virgin olive oil

⅓ cup panko bread crumbs

1 tablespoon minced fresh Italian parsley leaves

1 lemon, cut into wedges

1. Preheat the oven to 400°F.

2. Lay the shrimp out in one layer on a foil-lined sheet pan. Season them with salt and pepper. Cut butter into chunks and distribute around the shrimp. Sprinkle the red pepper, garlic, and shallot over the shrimp. Drizzle with olive oil. Scatter the bread crumbs on top.

3. Roast in oven for 10 to 15 minutes, until the shrimp are pink and cooked through and bread crumbs are golden.

4. Transfer to a serving dish. Sprinkle parsley and serve with lemon wedges.

PAIR WITH: Spaghetti with Spicy Aglio e Olio (page 60)

Fisherman's Seafood Stew with Shrimp, Clams, and Couscous

SERVES: 4 to 6 | **PREP TIME:** 10 minutes | **COOK TIME:** 25 minutes

This fisherman's stew is Sicilian-inspired. The mixture of fillet fish and shellfish speaks to the coast of Sicily, where fisherman bring in a wide variety of seafood. Because of Sicily's diverse history (it has been ruled by the Greeks, Normans, Arabs, and Spanish), Sicilian dishes have multicultural origins. The use of saffron in this recipe has Arab roots, and the stew is served on a bed of couscous, a direct connection to North Africa, which lies about 100 miles across from the southern coast of Sicily. Serve this with slices of crusty bread to soak up all the delicious broth.

¼ cup extra-virgin olive oil

1 medium onion, peeled and diced

2 garlic cloves, peeled and sliced

1 (28-ounce) can diced tomatoes

1 cup dry white wine

2 or 3 sprigs fresh thyme and/or fresh oregano

¼ teaspoon saffron threads

Salt

Freshly ground black pepper

4 (2-ounce) cod fillets

½ pound shrimp, shelled and deveined

3 dozen mussels, rinsed and debearded

2 tablespoons extra-virgin olive oil, plus more for drizzling

1½ cups quick-cooking couscous

1. Heat the oil in a large pot or Dutch oven that can hold all the ingredients. Sauté the onion and garlic until softened, 2 to 3 minutes. Add tomatoes, white wine, thyme or oregano, and saffron. Season with salt and pepper. Bring to a simmer and cook for 4–5 minutes.

2. Add the cod, shrimp, and mussels. Cover to steam on medium heat for 3 to 4 minutes. Stir ingredients, cover again, and cook at a lively simmer until shrimp and cod are opaque and mussels have opened, 8 to 10 minutes more.

3. Meanwhile, in a sauté pan with at least 2-inch sides, heat 1½ cups of water with 2 tablespoons olive oil and season with salt. Once liquid simmers, remove from heat. Add couscous, gently spreading out the grains evenly. Cover and let couscous stand to absorb water for about 10 minutes.

4. Fluff couscous with a fork, separating the grains well. Add a little olive oil. Stir to combine.

5. Spoon some couscous into serving bowls. Top with spoonfuls of fish and broth. Serve hot.

PAIR WITH: Riviera Focaccia with Rosemary and Olives (page 83)

Lightly Fried Calamari

SERVES: 4 to 6 | **PREP TIME:** 10 minutes | **COOK TIME:** 10 minutes

Calamari is squid. Most fish markets sell squid already cleaned, or you can ask them to clean it for you. There is a thin film of skin that needs to be removed, a thin bone in the center, and a "beak." The body of the squid is cut into rings, and the tentacles are left whole. Because of its strange appearance, when I was young, my family used to call calamari rings and tentacles "rubber bands and spiders."

1 pound squid, cleaned

2 cups canola oil

½ cup all-purpose flour

½ cup cornstarch

Salt

Freshly ground black pepper

1 lemon, thinly sliced (for garnish)

1 tablespoon minced fresh parsley leaves (for garnish)

1. Separate tentacle section from squid body. Slice squid body into ½-inch rings. Keep tentacles whole, or cut in half lengthwise.

2. Heat the oil to about 350 degrees in a heavy-bottomed medium pot or pan. You can tell it's hot enough if you drop in a small piece of bread and it bubbles and rises to the top.

3. Meanwhile, in a medium mixing bowl, whisk together flour and cornstarch; season with salt and pepper.

4. Dredge squid in the flour mixture and lift out some of it with a slotted spoon, tapping the spoon with your hand to get rid of excess flour. Carefully lower squid into hot oil. Cook for 1 to 2 minutes until golden. Remove with slotted spoon to paper-towel-lined plate. Repeat with the rest of the squid.

5. Season fried calamari with salt. Garnish with lemon and parsley. Serve hot.

INGREDIENT TIP: Calamari can quickly go from raw to overcooked. To avoid rubbery, too-tough results, make sure your pan is hot and don't cook the calamari longer than directed.

PAIR WITH: Clams Oreganata (page 20)

Steamed Mussels with Cannellini Beans and Bacon

SERVES: 4 to 6 | **PREP TIME:** 15 minutes | **COOK TIME:** 15 minutes

The idea of cooking with mussels can be daunting, but actually, they are quite easy to prepare. Mussels, known as bivalves or mollusks, cling together on seaweed along coastlines. They create a weblike material that you'll sometimes find along the edge of the shell. It's called the beard, and you need to tug this off the mussel before cooking. Most farm-raised mussels don't have beards. Mussels cook quickly; you know they're done when they open up while simmering. Discard any mussels that stay clamped shut after cooking.

6 slices bacon

2 tablespoons extra-virgin olive oil

1 small onion, peeled and diced

2 garlic cloves, peeled and minced

1 cup cannellini beans, drained and rinsed

½ cup dry white wine

Leaves from 4 or 5 sprigs Italian parsley, minced

Leaves from 4 or 5 sprigs tarragon, minced

2 pounds mussels, cleaned and debearded

1. Preheat the oven to 400°F.

2. Line a sheet pan with foil. Add a rack insert to the pan if you have one. Or just use the surface of the foil. Lay the bacon strips flat and roast in oven until cooked through and crispy, about 15 minutes. Let bacon drain on paper towels.

3. Heat the olive oil in a large saucepan. Add onion and garlic. Cook until softened and simmering, 2 to 3 minutes. Add the beans; stir to coat with oil; heat for 1 to 2 minutes. Add wine. When bubbling, add mussels, plus parsley and tarragon. Cover, cooking on medium-high heat for 8 to 10 minutes, until mussels have all opened (discard mussels that do not open after cooking).

4. Transfer mussels and their juices to a serving bowl. Crumble bacon slices over dish. Serve warm.

VARIATION TIP: If you enjoy this recipe and want to try something new, boil a half pound of spaghetti, drain it, and place it in a serving bowl. Pour the mussels and juices over it, and top with bacon.

PAIR WITH: Riviera Focaccia with Rosemary and Olives (page 83)

Dairy-Free

Easy Crab Cakes

SERVES: 4 to 6 | **PREP TIME:** 15 minutes, plus 30 minutes to chill | **COOK TIME:** 20 minutes

When I was a kid, we lived on the south shore of Long Island in New York. My family loved shellfish, and it was easy to find fresh shellfish in our area, but we loved to go out and catch blue-claw crabs ourselves. We'd fish at night, just along the docks of Great South Bay. With a strong flashlight and a scoop net, we'd see them swimming near the dock pylons and scoop them up out of the water. It was a wrestling match to clean live crabs, and a project to eat them, pulling small pieces of succulent meat from the shells—but, oh, so good. Thankfully, you can buy wonderful blue-crab meat in a container at the store. Look for "lump" crab meat; this is meat from the best part of the crab.

1 pound lump crab meat
(such as Phillips brand)

¾ cup panko bread crumbs

1 egg

1 tablespoon
Worcestershire sauce

1 tablespoon creamy
mustard, i.e., Dijon

½ cup mayonnaise

1 teaspoon celery
salt, or 1 teaspoon
Old Bay Seasoning

1 tablespoon minced
Italian parsley leaves

Salt

Freshly ground
black pepper

1. Preheat the oven to 375°F.

2. Add the crab to a large mixing bowl. Gently pick through the crab to find any pieces of shell.

3. Add bread crumbs and a little salt. Gently toss to coat, being careful not to break up lumps of meat.

4. In a separate medium mixing bowl, stir together egg, Worcestershire sauce, mustard, mayonnaise, celery salt, and parsley until smooth. Season with salt and pepper. Gently fold creamy mixture into crab, being careful not to break up lumps.

5. Line a sheet pan with parchment. Using 2 tablespoons, shape 1- to 2-inch balls into small mounds of crab mixture onto the sheet pan. Chill in refrigerator for about 30 minutes. Remove and gently press crab balls into lightly flattened cakes.

6. Bake for about 20 minutes until golden.

VARIATION TIP: Alternatively, pan-fry crab cakes in a little olive oil. Some store-bought cocktail sauce or tartar sauce is a nice addition for a condiment.

PAIR WITH: Amalfi Lemony Tuna Capellini (page 64)

Chocolate Tiramisu,
page 126

10

Pastries and Desserts

Italy is famous for its desserts, and in this chapter you will learn simple ways to re-create some of the country's most popular confections. Take two of the most iconic Italian treats—cannoli and tiramisu—for example. Since the fried dough casings of cannoli can be tricky to master, I use puff pastry instead to save time and effort (see page 130). And, in addition to a chocolatey spin on classic tiramisu (page 126), I've included a quicker, deconstructed version that tastes just as good (page 137).

Additionally, since fruit, cookies, and pastries are the desserts enjoyed in everyday Italian life, you'll find that more casual treats make up the bulk of this chapter. One of my favorites is the Rustic Peach Galette with Almond-Nutmeg Topping on page 133, an impressive tart that comes together quickly with very little work. The Sicilian Almond-Orange Cookies on page 131 are a direct connection to Sicily, where almonds and oranges grow in abundance. And then there's the Italian coffee bar favorite, cornetti—crescent-shaped goodies enjoyed for breakfast throughout Italy. No matter what kind of sweet you're craving, you will find the solution here in this chapter.

Chocolate Tiramisu

SERVES: 4 to 6 | **PREP TIME:** 25 minutes | **COOK TIME:** 1 hour to chill

This is a very light version of tiramisu. Traditionally, tiramisu is made with raw eggs. For this recipe, I've omitted the eggs, because the mascarpone-cream mixture is lavish enough. It requires making whipped cream. You can use a whisk to do this, but a hand mixer or stand mixer (if you have one) will make the process faster. Alternatively, you can buy whipped cream already made. The ladyfingers are cookies sometimes called *savoiardi*. They are *crunchy* ladyfingers (not the soft, cakey kind). These cookies become softened with the coffee mixture. You can find them in specialty food markets and some supermarkets.

1½ cups heavy cream

⅓ cup powdered sugar

1 pound mascarpone

1 teaspoon orange extract

3–4 tablespoons milk

¾ cup mini chocolate chips

⅓ cup instant espresso powder

5 teaspoons sugar, or to taste

¼ cup Orangecello, or favorite liqueur

½ cup unsweetened cocoa, divided

40 crunchy ladyfingers

1. Beat cream to soft peaks. Add powdered sugar; beat again until stiff peaks form.

2. In a separate large bowl, mix together the mascarpone and orange extract. Add a few tablespoons of milk to soften. Stir in chocolate chips. Gently fold in whipped cream.

3. In a shallow pan or container, combine espresso powder with 3 cups boiling water. Add 4 or 5 teaspoons sugar, or to taste. Stir until coffee and sugar are dissolved. Add 2 more cups of cool water. Add Orangecello. Mix to combine. Let cool.

4. Use a 9-by-13-inch shallow serving pan or casserole dish. Dip the ladyfingers into the coffee mixture one or two at a time, letting them soak up the coffee, but not so much that they fall apart. Place them in a single layer lined up against each other, 2 by 2.

5. Spread half the cream mixture evenly on top. Dust with half the cocoa to cover. Layer with a second layer of coffee-dipped ladyfingers. Top with the remaining cream; dust with remaining cocoa.

6. Chill for at least 1 hour, or overnight, before cutting into squares and serving.

INGREDIENT TIP: Orangecello is the orange version of *limoncello*—a sweet liqueur with the flavor of lemon (or orange). The coffee mixture is typically spiked with a sweet liqueur. Feel free to use your favorite or what you might have on hand. Sambuca, Cointreau, or amaretto are all good choices.

SERVE AFTER: Risotto Milanese with Saffron (page 48)

DESSERT CREAM

Cream is a recurring ingredient in many of these desserts, and it comes in many forms: whipped cream, ricotta cream, mascarpone, and creamy chocolate ganache.

Whipped cream is made from heavy cream. You can find heavy cream in any supermarket—it whips up easily and holds its shape for a day or more. Fresh-made whipped cream has the best flavor, but to save time, you can always use store-bought whipped cream for recipes like Mixed Berry Polenta Cobbler with Whipped Cream (page 128).

Ricotta cream is the filling for cannoli. Italian desserts often use sweetened ricotta, made creamier by mixing in a little milk. It's the other side to the cheese's personality, since you also find ricotta in many savory dishes.

Mascarpone is a key ingredient in Chocolate Tiramisu (page 126), where it's folded into whipped cream to make a luscious, sweet layer of the dessert. Mascarpone is also the decadent filling in Raspberry-Mascarpone Mini Hand Pies (page 135). Its consistency is like cream cheese, but it has a sweeter, less tangy taste.

Chocolate ganache makes Espresso-Poached Pears with Chocolate Sauce (page 136) sublime. Ganache is an easy, exceptional topping made by mixing melted chocolate with heavy cream.

Mixed Berry Polenta Cobbler with Whipped Cream

SERVES: 4 to 6 | **PREP TIME:** 25 minutes | **COOK TIME:** 25 minutes

A cobbler-style dessert is so comforting and can be put together quickly. Usually there's a biscuit-like topping on top of the fruit, but here I've added a tasty Italian flare to this topping by incorporating cornmeal. It gives the cobbler a lighter, polenta-like touch. You can use any mixture of berries for the fruit. In this recipe I chose strawberries and blueberries, but feel free to try blackberries or raspberries, too. Or substitute sliced peaches, nectarines, apricots, plums, or even cherries (remove the pits first).

You might choose your fruit according to the season. You can even increase the amount of fruit to change the ratio of fruit to topping.

FOR THE FRUIT FILLING

2 cups hulled, sliced strawberries

2 cups blueberries

½ cup sugar

1 tablespoon all-purpose flour

FOR THE POLENTA TOPPING

1 cup flour

½ cup cornmeal

2 teaspoons baking powder

1 teaspoon baking soda

2 tablespoons sugar, plus more for sprinkling

1 stick unsalted butter, cut into small chunks

¾ cup plain yogurt, preferably Greek yogurt

½ cup milk

FOR THE CREAM

1 cup heavy cream

3 tablespoons powdered sugar

¼ teaspoon vanilla extract

TO MAKE THE FRUIT FILLING

1. Preheat the oven to 375°F.

2. In a medium mixing bowl gently stir together the strawberries, blueberries, sugar, and flour until well combined. Distribute fruit filling to cover the bottom of a 9-by-13-inch baking or casserole pan.

TO MAKE THE POLENTA TOPPING

1. Place the flour, cornmeal, baking powder, baking soda, and sugar into a large mixing bowl. Whisk to combine well. Add the butter and cut it into the flour mixture, with a pastry cutter or 2 knives, until the butter is broken down into very small pieces. Add the yogurt and milk. Stir to combine until smooth.

2. Spoon the mixture in large dollops over the fruit until it's almost covered. Flatten batter gently. Sprinkle with a little extra sugar. Bake for about 25 minutes until polenta is golden brown and fruit is bubbling.

TO MAKE THE CREAM

Meanwhile, make the whipped cream. Beat the cream with powdered sugar and vanilla until medium peaks form, using a whisk or a hand mixer. Serve cobbler warm or at room temperature with a dollop of whipped cream on each serving.

VARIATION TIP: Store-bought whipped cream works with this recipe, too, but fresh whipped cream is really special. If you have a food processor, you can save a little time by pulsing the polenta ingredients until smooth.

SERVE AFTER: Spice-Rubbed Pork Tenderloin (page 106)

Puff Pastry Cannoli with Sweet Ricotta Cream

SERVES: 4 to 6 | **PREP TIME:** 25 minutes | **COOK TIME:** 30 minutes

When you think of Italian desserts, cannoli are often the first treat that comes to mind. These traditional pastries from Sicily capture the crunch and creaminess of Italian sweets. Usually, you have to make a special dough and deep-fry the shells. But here's a lighter, quicker version using store-bought puff pastry. One particular piece of equipment is needed, though: cannoli tubes. They are thin, metal tubes that create the shape of the crusts. You can find them in specialty housewares stores or online.

1 sheet puff pastry, defrosted

3 tablespoons unsalted butter

1 egg, lightly beaten with 1 teaspoon of water

2½ cups ricotta

½ cup sugar

2 or 3 tablespoons heavy cream

⅓ cup shelled pistachios or walnuts, crushed

¼ cup powdered sugar

1. Preheat the oven to 350°F.

2. Roll out dough on a lightly floured surface until pretty thin (increase the rectangle to about 30 percent larger). Cut dough widthwise into 1-inch strips.

3. Coat the cannoli tubes with a thin film of butter. Gently but firmly wrap a strip of dough around a tube, making an overlapping spiral. Don't pull the dough too tightly to wrap, but gently secure. Repeat with the rest of the dough and tubes. Place seam-side down on a parchment-lined baking sheet. Lightly brush with egg wash. Bake for about 30 minutes until golden. When cool enough to handle, very gently slide the pastry off the form. Let cool completely before filling.

4. In a medium mixing bowl, combine the ricotta with sugar and whisk until sugar no longer feels gritty. Stir in the cream if the mixture feels very thick (you may not need it). Spoon half of the mixture into a quart-size ziplock bag. Push mixture to a bottom corner and seal the bag, pressing out air. Snip the corner where the ricotta is, creating a hole about the size of a pea.

5. Hold one of the pastries upright and place the pastry bag 1 or 2 inches from the opening at the top. Squeeze the bag, filling the pastry form with the ricotta. Press crushed nuts at either end. Repeat with the rest of the pastry and filling. Place on a serving platter. Dust with powdered sugar. Serve right away or refrigerate overnight.

TECHNIQUE TIP: If cannoli tubes are hard to find, you can simulate the tube by rolling up parchment paper into solid cylinders.

SERVE AFTER: Eggplant Parmigiana (page 92)

Sicilian Almond-Orange Cookies

SERVES: 4 to 6 | **PREP TIME:** 15 minutes | **COOK TIME:** 12 minutes

Our Sicilian cooking teacher in Palermo made these cookies in the blink of an eye. My group and I were cooking in the galley of a pleasure boat in Palermo harbor. After preparing a full fish feast, these cookies were a beautiful perfect treat for dessert. Almonds are grown in Sicily and show up all throughout Sicilian cuisine.

2 cups almond flour

1 cup sugar

¼ teaspoon orange extract

3 egg whites

1 cup crushed almonds

1 dozen candied or maraschino cherries, quartered

1. Preheat the oven to 400°F.

2. In a medium mixing bowl, whisk together the almond flour and sugar. Stir in the orange extract and egg whites and mix until a dough forms. Knead to combine.

3. Pull off a small amount of dough and roll into a 1-inch ball. Roll each ball in the crushed almonds, press a piece of quartered cherry on top, and place on a parchment-lined baking sheet. Repeat with the rest of the dough (makes about 1 dozen).

4. Bake for about 12 minutes until golden.

INGREDIENT TIP: Look for almond flour in most supermarkets. Organic markets, Trader Joe's, Costco, and specialty gourmet stores also carry it.

SERVE AFTER: Penne with Roasted Cherry Tomato Sauce (page 67)

Puff Pastry Cornetto with Marmalade

SERVES: 4 to 6 | **PREP TIME:** 15 minutes | **COOK TIME:** 15 minutes

Breakfast at an Italian bar always includes *cornetti* (plural for *cornetto*). They are crescent-shaped pastries, similar to croissants—*cornetto* means "little horn." The bar counter typically displays a variety of filled *cornetti: marmelatta* (marmalade), *crema* (cream), *cioccalato* (chocolate), or *vuoto* (empty and plain). It's my very favorite way to spend an Italian morning, eating a *cornetto*— wrapped in a piece of wax paper to hand-hold—and drinking cappuccino. This recipe is an easy, homemade version of the Italian treat, and great for dessert, too.

1 sheet frozen puff pastry, thawed

Flour for dusting work surface

¾ cup apricot jam, or your favorite marmalade or jam

2 or 3 tablespoons milk

2 or 3 tablespoons sugar

1. Preheat the oven to 400°F.

2. Dust a clean work surface with a little flour. Roll out the puff pastry sheet to about ⅛-inch thick. Cut into 6 squares. Cut each square down the middle diagonally to create 2 triangles for each square.

3. Place a tablespoon of jam at the wide side of a triangle. Roll up, from the wide side, to create a crescent-roll shape, turning down the corners to make the crescent. Place on a parchment-lined sheet pan. Repeat with rest of dough.

4. Brush each crescent with milk. Sprinkle with sugar. Bake for 15 minutes until golden.

TECHNIQUE TIP: The recipe creates 12 small *cornetti*. For larger ones, cut dough into four squares, which will make 8 triangles.

SERVE AFTER: Soft and Cheesy Polenta with Roasted Mushrooms (page 40)

Rustic Peach Galette with Almond-Nutmeg Topping

SERVES: 4 to 6 | **PREP TIME:** 15 minutes, plus 1 hour inactive time for chilling dough | **COOK TIME:** 35 minutes

Galette is a French term for a free-form tart. Italians use the term, too, but also call free-form tarts *crostata*. *Crostata* can also be a tart that is cooked in a pie pan. But free-form is the key here. Once your dough is ready, you roll it out into a circle, or close to a circle shape. Pile your filling in the center, leaving a border, then just fold up your border over the edges of the fruit filling. No shaping or fitting into a pan; this dessert is the shape *you* make it. If you don't want to spend the time making the crust, store-bought pie dough will be perfect, too.

FOR THE CRUST

1 cup flour, plus more for dusting work surface

1 teaspoon sugar

Pinch salt

6 tablespoons cold unsalted butter, cut into cubes

Scant ¼ cup cold white wine, or ice water

FOR THE FILLING

4 or 5 peaches

⅓ cup sugar

2 short sprigs rosemary, leaves minced, stems discarded

2 teaspoons flour

½ cup sliced almonds, divided

1 egg, beaten with a teaspoon of water

½ teaspoon nutmeg

¼ cup brown sugar

TO MAKE THE CRUST

In a medium mixing bowl, whisk together the flour, sugar, and salt. Add the butter, and using two knives or a pastry cutter, cut butter into the flour into small pieces. Add wine, then mix gently with hands to blend into a ball of dough. Flatten into a thick disk, wrap in plastic, and refrigerate for about an hour.

TO MAKE THE FILLING

Peel the peaches, remove the pits, and cut into thin wedges. In a medium mixing bowl, stir together the peaches, sugar, rosemary, flour, and ¼ cup sliced almonds.

TO FINISH THE DESSERT

1. Preheat the oven to 375°F.

2. Roll out the dough on a lightly floured surface into a large circle or oblong, about ⅛-inch thick. Place rolled-out dough on a parchment-lined sheet pan. Place the filling in the center and spread it out, leaving at least a 2-inch border of dough. Fold the dough border over the filling, making small folds all around. Brush dough with egg wash.

3. Mix together the remaining ¼ cup of almonds with nutmeg and brown sugar. Sprinkle mixture on top of dough and filling. Bake for 30 to 35 minutes until the dough is golden and filling is bubbly

SERVE AFTER: Lemony Risotto with Asparagus (page 46)

Amaretto Chocolate Brownies with Walnuts

SERVES: 4 to 6 | **PREP TIME:** 15 minutes | **COOK TIME:** 40 minutes

These brownies are spiked with amaretto, an almond-flavored Italian liqueur, and also almond extract, transforming the usual brownie into something a little more grown-up. I also bring more nuts to the party by stirring in a cup of walnuts for their flavor and tender crunch.

1 stick (8 tablespoons) unsalted butter, plus more to grease the pan.

½ cup cocoa powder

2 eggs

1 teaspoon vanilla extract

½ teaspoon almond extract

2 tablespoons amaretto liqueur

⅔ cup sugar

¼ cup all-purpose flour

Pinch salt

1 cup chopped walnuts

1. Preheat the oven to 325°F. Lightly butter an 8-inch square baking pan.

2. Melt the butter in a small saucepan. Stir in the cocoa until smooth. Remove from heat and let cool a bit, about 2 minutes. Pour into a medium mixing bowl and whisk in the eggs, one at a time. Stir in the vanilla, almond extract, and amaretto.

3. In a separate bowl, whisk together the sugar, flour, and salt. Stir the dry ingredients into the wet ingredients. Mix until smooth. Stir in the walnuts.

4. Pour batter into the prepared pan and smooth the top. Bake for about 40 minutes. Let brownies cool before cutting into squares.

VARIATION TIP: If you don't have any amaretto in the house, try spiking these brownies with another favorite liqueur, like Fra Angelico (hazelnut-flavored), or Cointreau (orange-flavored).

SERVE AFTER: Spaghetti Cacio e Pepe (page 62)

Raspberry-Mascarpone Mini Hand Pies

SERVES: 4 to 6 | **PREP TIME:** 15 minutes, plus 1 hour inactive for dough to chill | **COOK TIME:** 20 minutes

I know some people shy away from making pie or tart dough. I used to be one of those people. But now that I know how to do it, I make it often and easily. It doesn't take a lot of time, and it has its rewards. It's tender and a little crusty. If you want to save time, you can make this recipe with store-bought puff pastry or pie dough—either will work just fine, too. The key ingredient is Italian mascarpone, that fabulous creamy, dense cheese that gives many Italian desserts their lusciousness.

FOR THE CRUST

1½ cups flour, plus more to dust work surface

1 teaspoon sugar

Pinch salt

1 stick cold, unsalted butter (8 tablespoons), cut into tablespoons

¼ cup chilled white wine

1 egg, lightly beaten with 1 teaspoon of water (for the egg wash)

FOR THE FILLING

⅓ cup sugar, plus 2 tablespoons, divided

8 ounces mascarpone, at room temperature

2 cups fresh raspberries

TO MAKE THE CRUST

Place the flour, sugar, and salt in a medium mixing bowl. Whisk to combine. Add the butter pieces, then using two knives, or a pastry cutter, cut butter into flour into pea-size pieces. Add wine; mix and knead gently with your hands just until a ball of dough forms. Flatten the ball into a disk, wrap in plastic, chill for 1 hour.

TO MAKE THE FILLING

In a medium mixing bowl, stir ⅓ cup of sugar and mascarpone together until smooth. Stir in raspberries.

TO FINISH THE DESSERT

1. Preheat the oven to 400°F.

2. Roll out dough onto floured surface to about ⅛-inch thick. Cut into 3-inch squares (or use a 3-inch biscuit cutter). Place a teaspoon or so of fruit-cheese mixture in the center of each square, and fold into a triangle. Press the edges together with fork tines. Brush each lightly with egg wash, and make a small slit in the top. Sprinkle sugar on top.

3. Place mini-pies on a parchment-lined sheet pan. Reroll leftover dough to make more. Bake for 20 minutes or until golden. Makes about 1 dozen.

TIME-SAVING TIP: If you have a food processor, you can make the dough in a snap. Add flour mixture, then butter. Pulse for a few seconds, then add the wine. Pulse until a ball of dough forms. Continue with the rest of the recipe.

SERVE AFTER: Roasted Salmon with Olives, Capers, and Herbs (page 116)

Espresso-Poached Pears with Chocolate Sauce

SERVES: 4 to 6 | **PREP TIME:** 15 minutes | **COOK TIME:** 30 minutes

Pears are one of the best fruits for poaching. Their shape holds up to simmering, and when you leave the stem on, you can serve the fruit standing up, which makes a lovely presentation. In this recipe we're poaching in espresso coffee–lemon liquid. The coffee will also tinge the pear to a tawny color. You can brew your own espresso, or use instant espresso (it comes in small jars in the coffee section of some markets). If you can't get your hands on some espresso, use regular coffee.

6 small to medium Bosc or Bartlett pears

2 or 3 cups espresso coffee (if using instant espresso coffee, use 3 teaspoons per 2 cups)

½ cup sugar

½ teaspoon vanilla extract

4 lemon peels

¾ cup chocolate chips (preferably bittersweet or semisweet)

½ cup heavy cream

1 teaspoon lemon zest

1. Peel the pears, leaving them whole with stems. If there are any that don't stand easily, cut a sliver from the bottom to make them flatter for standing.

2. In a large saucepan that is big enough to hold the pears standing up, combine the espresso, sugar, vanilla, and lemon peels. Place the pears in the pan, stem-side up, and pour in enough water to submerge all but their stems. Bring to a simmer. Simmer gently for about 30 minutes. Remove pears from the liquid and let them drain on a paper towel.

3. Meanwhile, make the chocolate sauce. Combine the chocolate chips and cream in a small saucepan over low heat, and stir until the chocolate is completely melted. Remove the pan from the heat as soon as the chocolate as melted, then stir in the lemon zest.

4. Serve individual pears with a drizzle of chocolate sauce.

SERVE AFTER: Linguine with Fra Diavolo Shrimp Sauce (page 68)

Quick Tiramisu with Biscotti and Mascarpone

SERVES: 4 to 6 | **PREP TIME:** 15 minutes

The word *tiramisu* translates to "pick me up." It's the kind of dessert that rounds out a meal with an excitement of sweetness. This recipe takes all the tiramisu wonders and transforms them into an abbreviated, concentrated version of its best flavors. For the biscotti cookies, choose any of your favorites—all varieties are perfect here.

8 ounces store-bought Italian biscotti cookies

½ cup rum (or your favorite spirit), divided

¼ cup brewed espresso coffee

8 ounces mascarpone

¼ cup sugar

⅓ cup chocolate chips

⅓ cup sliced almonds

1. Break up the cookies with a knife, into small bite-size pieces. Lay out broken cookies in one layer in a medium cake pan or casserole dish. Sprinkle ¼ cup of liquor evenly over cookies. Sprinkle the coffee evenly over the cookies.

2. In a medium mixing bowl, stir together the mascarpone, the remaining ¼ cup of liquor, and the sugar, until very smooth. Spoon dollops of mixture over cookies, then spread evenly with a spatula. Sprinkle chocolate chips and almonds.

3. Serve by spooning out mixture for individual servings.

SERVE AFTER: Chicken Piccata with Lemon and Capers (page 100)

Chocolate Tiramisu, page 126

Measurement Conversions

VOLUME EQUIVALENTS (LIQUID)

US STANDARD	US STANDARD (OUNCES)	METRIC (APPROXIMATE)
2 tablespoons	1 fl. oz.	30 mL
¼ cup	2 fl. oz.	60 mL
½ cup	4 fl. oz.	120 mL
1 cup	8 fl. oz.	240 mL
1½ cups	12 fl. oz.	355 mL
2 cups or 1 pint	16 fl. oz.	475 mL
4 cups or 1 quart	32 fl. oz.	1 L
1 gallon	128 fl. oz.	4 L

OVEN TEMPERATURES

FAHRENHEIT (F)	CELSIUS (C) (APPROXIMATE)
250° F	120° C
300° F	150° C
325° F	165° C
350° F	180° C
375° F	190° C
400° F	200° C
425° F	220° C
450° F	230° C

VOLUME EQUIVALENTS (DRY)

US STANDARD	METRIC (APPROXIMATE)
⅛ teaspoon	0.5 mL
¼ teaspoon	1 mL
½ teaspoon	2 mL
¾ teaspoon	4 mL
1 teaspoon	5 mL
1 tablespoon	15 mL
¼ cup	59 mL
⅓ cup	79 mL
½ cup	118 mL
⅔ cup	156 mL
¾ cup	177 mL
1 cup	235 mL
2 cups or 1 pint	475 mL
3 cups	700 mL
4 cups or 1 quart	1 L

WEIGHT EQUIVALENTS

US STANDARD	METRIC (APPROXIMATE)
½ ounce	15 g
1 ounce	30 g
2 ounces	60 g
4 ounces	115 g
8 ounces	225 g
12 ounces	340 g
16 ounces or 1 pound	455 g

Index

Acknowledgments

THERE ARE SO MANY WONDERFUL INFLUENCES ON MY ITALIAN COOKING. When I lived in Italy, and during my many trips to Italy, I had the good fortune to meet and cook with lovely people everywhere. Thank you, Gianna Greco in Lecce, Bruno Gianfrate in Martina Franca, Stefania Bertaccini in Parma, Chef Vincenzo in Ravello, Giuliana and Alessandro of Uncovered Sicily in Ragusa, Chef Marika Contaldo Seguso in Venice, Bianca Cingolani in Liguria, my Roman best friend, Malena McGrath, and my Roman roommate, Enrica Brunelli. In the States, many thanks to Micol Negrin of Rustico Cooking in New York. Thanks, too, to my extended family of Italian American relatives, whose influences are almost impossible to measure since they make up who I am (of course, especially my mom). All of the recipes in this book have been cooked over and over in my classes. Thank you to my fabulous students, who so enthusiastically embraced my recipes and made them their own.

About the Author

PAULETTE LICITRA has been teaching Italian cooking in Nashville, Tennessee, since 2009. She leads small groups to Italy every year to cook and explore regional cuisines. Paulette completed her professional culinary studies at the Institute of Culinary Education in New York City, and worked at Mario Batali's Lupa restaurant. She's studied with home cooks and chefs all over Italy, including the regions of Lazio, Campania, Sicily, Tuscany, Puglia, Liguria, Emilia-Romagna, and the Veneto. Paulette is also known as Chef Paulette and appears frequently on the Nashville NBC affiliate WSMV-TV. Her writing has appeared in the *New York Times*, *Chicago Tribune*, and other publications. Paulette was founder and publisher of the literary journal *Alimentum: The Literature of Food*. Her first cookbook, *Italian Cooking Party*, inspired cooks to host their own Italian cooking parties. She is a charter member of the Nashville chapter of Les Dames d'Escoffier. For more info, see ChefPaulette.net.

CPSIA information can be obtained
at www.ICGtesting.com
Printed in the USA
LVHW072235010821
694291LV00015B/1004